War and Faith

Short Biographies
from the Second World War

Don Stephens
Author of War and Grace

€P

EP BOOKS

1st Floor Venture House, 6 Silver Court, Watchmead,
Welwyn Garden City, UK, AL7 1TS

web: http://www.epbooks.org

e-mail: sales@epbooks.org

EP Books are distributed in the USA by:
JPL Distribution
3741 Linden Avenue Southeast
Grand Rapids, MI 49548
E-mail: orders@jpldistribution.com
Tel: 877.683.6935

British Library Cataloguing in Publication Data available

ISBN: 978-1-78397-150-3

To my wife Hazel,
my daughter Heather,
and son-in-law Mark,
with love and thanks

ABOUT THE FRONT COVER

It was 14 October 1940. The air raid sirens had sounded. They indicated that a large German night raid, part of the 'Blitz', was in progress. German bombers had been ordered to aim at the London docks. During this raid George Hitchin was driving his no.88 double-decker bus very cautiously in total blackout conditions along Balham High Road in south London.

At exactly 8.02 pm a German 1400 kg. bomb exploded only 25 yards (23 metres) ahead of his bus. It was totally impossible to avoid the crater and the bus went straight into it. All the passengers survived, though George Hitchin was knocked unconscious and received help at the first aid post in Du Cane Road.

More seriously, the bomb penetrated into the tunnel of the Northern Underground Line at Balham Station. The two platforms of the underground system were linked by a passage 32 feet (10 metres) deep. Filled with rubble, this space was largely responsible for trapping those who had become casualties. Gas and water pipes were fractured and the blast and flooding caused over 60 deaths. The damage to Balham tube station was so severe that the electric trains could not use the lines until January 1941.

Contents

Foreword

This book contains short biographies of Christian men and one remarkable Christian woman. They come from a wide variety of different countries, including South Africa, USA, England, Scotland, Holland, Germany and Poland. These believers were involved in a very large range of situations and responsibilities during the war. Most were brought to saving faith before the outbreak of the Second World War—and two shortly afterwards. Every account testifies to the power of God to save and keep people in testing circumstances.

The accounts include unusual experiences and are full of godly living, adventure and courage. The reader will note that the author has been thorough and diligent in his research and in several cases has had extended and direct communication with his subject. He has the gift of telling a story in a way which grips the reader, and yet he is not guilty of writing in a sensational manner, nor does he fail to remind his reader that war is always a terrible event, and that the God of the Bible remains sovereign.

Those who have taken the trouble to acquire this admirable work will benefit spiritually from reading it. They will not be surprised to learn that this book is a requested sequel to *War and Grace*, first published in 2005. It is to be fervently hoped that this new title will find the same wide readership as his earlier work.

It can be recommended without any reservation.

BRIGADIER IAN DOBBIE, OBE,
Chairman of SASRA 1991–2013

Preface

The Second World War was the most destructive conflict in human history. In the 2,174 days between Germany's attack on Poland in September 1939 and the surrender of Japan in August 1945 well over forty million people died. Some say that sixty million would be a more accurate figure. Nobody will ever know for certain. And who can calculate the millions who suffered wounds, pain, mental scars and all kinds of loss?

This book tells the stories of eight people and their experiences before, during, and in the years following World War II. Several of them were caught up in the cruel persecution of the Jewish people by the Nazis. Others were actively involved in the fight to defeat the evil ideology which led to such atrocities. All of these people came to a living faith in Christ, and from then on their faith was the driving force behind their lives. Whether the reader is a Christian believer or not, I hope that these true accounts will prove interesting and challenging, perhaps even life-changing.

The book is also intended as a sequel to one which I wrote in 2005 called *War and Grace*. The same approach is adopted in the narration, and the motivation behind the writing is the same for both books. However, interested readers and reviewers need to be reminded that though there are similarities, there are enforced differences. One such difference is the limited amount of suitable material which is available about this horrendous war. I could find no unused Japanese, French, Russian or other writings which were relevant to my theme. The scope of the narratives is, therefore, necessarily governed by the sources now available. Most readers will know of someone who in their opinion could be included in a book of this type. I am in the same position, but many such people are either very well known, or the reverse is true—there is not enough information about them to write a full biography.

My ambition is the same as that of the apostle John. At the end of the Gospel bearing his name we read these words: '... these are written that you may believe that Jesus is the Christ, the Son of God, and that believing you may have life in his name' (John 20:31).

DON STEPHENS

Acknowledgements

Nobody writes a book alone.

This book was in my mind for nearly ten years before I sat down and wrote it. During that time I received over 500 images, the precise origin of which is now sometimes uncertain. I have tried very hard to track down the suppliers. If I have used material and not credited it adequately, it will be a mistake for which I hope I may be graciously forgiven. Should this book ever be reprinted it will present an opportunity to correct errors of this type. Perhaps readers need to be reminded that many pictures are very old, so the modern quality we have come to expect is often impossible given the low resolution of the originals.

Many acknowledgements, both for purchased and other images, as well as various textual references, are credited at the end of each chapter in the sections called MORE INFORMATION ON … However, in addition to those named in this way, there are many other kind friends who deserve acknowledgement. Some made comparatively small contributions; others sacrificed many hours of their time and expertise. In alphabetical order they are: Mircea Aioanei, K. Paul Austin, Jan Bradford, Phil Butler, John Davison, Ian Dobbie, Jakub Gościnny, Arthur Howe, Gwyneth Jones, Arthur Kulcsar, Tim Leung, Mike Lewis, Roy Mason, Vic Mitchell, Marjorie Peters, David Poll, Mike Shaw, Vikky Skinner, David Smith, Pam Stevens, Waldemar Tański, Jean Vann, Graham Ward, Brian Williams and Anne Williamson.

Thank you all and forgive me if I have omitted your name. In addition, I acknowledge the current staff of the publisher led by Graham Hind.

Quite a few stories never made it into the book, but a lot of hard work was done, often by me, before a final decision about omission was made. In this connection I thank Jonathan Wells for his work relating to Canon Clifford Cohu. This brave citizen of the Channel Islands was put to death by the Nazis. His challenge to the Germans during his retirement is well documented, but if anybody should read this and could shed light on his long career in India before the Second World War, I ask them to contact me via the publisher.

DON STEPHENS

1

Steve Stevens:
War hero and pioneer missionary pilot

As the end of the Second World War approached, the Allied war effort reached a crescendo. The Nazis were on the run. Defeat stared them in the face. The Allied Air Forces had played a crucial role in bringing about this state of affairs and, with the cessation of hostilities in the not-too-distant future, the thoughts of a number of airmen began to turn to the possibility of a new application for the flying skills which they had learned. Instead of spreading death and destruction, why not use aircraft to bring life and hope?

These airmen came from various countries, including Britain, the United States, Australia and South Africa. They had arrived at this conclusion independently of one another, but they shared the same desire, and in most cases the same Christian faith. All of them knew that some organization would have to take place. Embryonic plans emerged in different ways in the countries involved. The unifying factor among them all was the basic idea: instead of being weapons of war, aircraft could be used for peaceful humanitarian purposes.

One such airman was Lieutenant Steve J. Stevens, DFC, of the South African Air Force (SAAF). He had been thinking along these lines for some years before he finally made the decision in 1950 to resign his SAAF commission in order to become a pilot on the staff of a newly formed organization called Mission Aviation Fellowship (UK).

Early Life

Steve Stevens was born in August 1919, the only son of a regular British army officer. His father, Captain George Stevens, who had served in the First World War, had been gassed while in Salonika. As a regular soldier Steve's father remained in the army. During his first ten years, Steve's family lived the typical life of the military. One short posting

Steve with his father

followed another, punctuated by periods of official sick leave caused by mustard gas. Steve's education in those years was a casualty. There were some short spells in school. Occasionally some inadequate home-schooling took place. The left-handed boy even became victim to the theory that he should be forced to use his right hand for written work. His father did his best to help him, but by the time he was ten, he had lived in five countries. No consecutive education was possible.

In 1929 George Stevens received news of his next posting. The family was scheduled to move to India. The army medical officer intervened. His opinion was that George Stevens should be invalided out of the army, and advised a move to a more congenial climate. As a result, he emigrated to South Africa with his wife and son, where he bought a farm. The professional soldier had become a farmer.

In 1934 the family suffered a heavy blow. Steve's mother, Dora, died after an unsuccessful operation for a brain tumour. It was especially hard for a fourteen-year-old boy to accept. His mother's long illness was to have unforeseen and life-changing consequences for the whole family. Steve's father had no time for Christians, whom he referred to disparagingly as 'Bible Thumpers'. However, when his wife needed medical care, the only doctor nearby was a Christian, Dr Barton, a Scottish medical missionary working in the area, mainly among the Zulus.

Up to that time, George Stevens knew almost nothing about the Bible or Christianity. The attitude was that, if God existed at all, so long as he led a 'good' life that would be enough to please him. What else could he expect? However, through regular contact with Dr Barton and other missionaries, who supported the family through Dora Stevens' illness, George began to see his need for a personal faith in a personal God.

Eventually, Steve's father decided to attend a church service. The preacher was an Australian Congregational minister named Lionel Fletcher who explained clearly the basis of real faith: how Christ had died to save the ungodly, and how the Holy Spirit gave new life and hope. George Stevens came to God in God's way—by prayer which admitted his own sinfulness, and by putting his faith in Christ alone for salvation. From that point on, his life was totally changed.

Something else was also to change. In 1937 George married one of the Scottish missionaries. Margaret Stevens became Steve's stepmother. She was the mother of Steve's two half sisters and a half brother.

The Call of God

Although the observable changes in his father's life-style made a small impression on Steve, it did not persuade him of the truth of the Christian faith. He captures his thoughts in the period after the change in his father with these words, 'At that time in my life, I had never been to a church service or attended a Sunday school. Nor had I ever been taught anything about Christianity—or any other religion for that matter.' He felt distinctly uneasy whenever the missionaries visited the farmhouse. They were still 'Bible Thumpers' as far as he was concerned. Surely their primary reason for being there was to help the Zulus, not him?

Then his father invited some of the missionaries to stay in the farmhouse while they conducted a series of meetings explaining their work. During the course of his stay, one of them, Adam Ferguson, asked Steve to show him the Oribi Gorge. This was an interesting geographical feature on the edge of the family farmland. Steve wrote, 'In all courtesy I could not refuse. I was happy to show him the Gorge, but was reluctant to spend time alone with him in case he talked about his faith.'

During the foray to the Oribi Gorge and back, Adam Ferguson quoted one of the most well-known verses in the Bible. The teaching in it was new to the fifteen-year-old Steve. It said, 'For God so loved the world that he gave his only begotten Son, that whosoever believeth in him should not perish, but have everlasting life.' Adam Ferguson persisted, 'If that verse is true, it applies to you. Don't you think you should do something about it?' 'Yes', conceded Steve, 'but what?' The response was, 'Thank the Lord for coming to die for you. Tell

Adam Ferguson with his wife, Isabelle

him that you want to receive him as your Saviour from the penalty of sin, and that you will turn from your sin and live for him.' Steve understood the gospel for the first time. The call of God came to his heart with the power of an irresistible lightning bolt.

Steve described what happened next as follows: 'At a very deep and real level, and not because it was expected of me, but because it was what I wanted, I knelt down by the sofa in my house, and prayed to Christ to be my Saviour … that decision was a turning point for me; a moment of time that revolutionized the whole of my life.'

For many months after this, his ingrained habits such as swearing, blasphemy, and continual lying continued. His former way of life without God had gone, but even with God he was far from perfect. Reminiscing, he recalled that after coming out with a mouthful of blasphemy, he was encouraged to be told of a biblical promise that had been written primarily to believers, and that meant him. It was, 'If we confess our sins, he is faithful and just to forgive us our sins, and to cleanse us from all unrighteousness' (1

John 1:9). He could understand from this verse that real Christians struggled with wrongdoing, just as he found it hard at first to give up blasphemous swearing and lying.

Beginning with the prayer, uttered in his teens, and throughout his life from that point onwards, God has always been real to him and he has been conscious of God's presence. As with all Christians, he has made mistakes, but he knows the joy of sins forgiven through faith in the crucified and risen Christ. Those who fought and worked with him in later life knew him as a man of faith, and respected him as such.

The Second World War

Steve worked on the farm full-time from the age of sixteen. However, at nineteen, eager to add to his education, he enrolled in The Bible Institute of South Africa in Cape Town. His time there ended abruptly in August 1940. The Battle of Britain was at its height. Although there was no conscription in South Africa, thousands of young men from that country were determined to help Britain in its hour of need. Those who were of Dutch ancestry were incensed that the Nazis had overrun the neutral Netherlands, while others who came from a British background read about the Blitz on Britain, heard Churchill's defiant speeches, and were keen to help the only country which was actively fighting Nazi power at that point in time. The Bible Institute was closed down for the duration of the war simply because nearly all the students joined the armed services. Steve was one of them.

Dreaming of flying a Spitfire, Steve enrolled in the South African Air Force. On a cold winter morning in June 1941, he made his first flight in a yellow-painted Tiger Moth. After ten hours of tuition, he flew solo. He could not know that by the end of his flying career he would have accumulated about 4000 hours in the air as a pilot. Few airmen gain such vast experience.

Having qualified as a pilot, Steve hoped for a posting to fly fighter aircraft. Perhaps his dream of finding himself at the controls of a Spitfire still lingered in his mind. It was a bitter disappointment to him that instead he was sent to learn how to be a flying instructor. Britain was short of aircrew and

South Africa had agreed to be part of the Empire Air Training Scheme. Men like Steve were needed to mould trainees into crew members for the RAF. Although it was with a heavy heart that he undertook this task, he proved to be an effective instructor. He even had to undergo the frustration of seeing one of the men whom he had taught to fly go on to be a Spitfire pilot—the very thing that he himself was longing to do!

Action at Last

Then things changed. In the late summer of 1944, he was posted to 19 Squadron of the SAAF, part of the Balkan Air Force. The squadron was based at Biferno, about halfway up Italy's Adriatic coast near Campomarino. One of their major tasks was to support the secret army of partisans as they fought against the hated Nazis in former Yugoslavia. Another was to keep the Adriatic Sea free from German shipping. Their Beaufighter aircraft were twin-engine planes, which had four rockets under each wing as well as cannons mounted within the wings. In all Steve flew thirty-five missions in Beaufighters. These risky operations only ended when Germany surrendered in May 1945.

A Beaufighter over the sea

One of his first actions in support of the Yugoslav guerrilla fighters was to destroy a Nazi barracks at Bjelovar. During the action a shell hit the windscreen of his Beaufighter. If there had not been a pane of armoured glass directly in front of the pilot's head, he would have been killed. As he graphically expressed it, 'I would have had no head'.

On 13 February 1945 Steve's squadron was ordered to attack the Nazi stronghold of Žužemberk in Slovenia. The photograph opposite is of Steve's Beaufighter in action during this attack and was to become one of the Second World War's most memorable rocket action images. It was taken

Steve's Beaufighter in action

by Steve Schonveld, the pilot of the plane immediately behind him, using a camera mounted in the nose of his aircraft.

Flying Beaufighters on low-level attacks was very dangerous. The casualty figures in all such actions are inevitably high. One bullet or shell in the wrong place could cause a fatal outcome. For instance, during an attack in which Steve took part on Cernik Castle, which was being used as a German headquarters, the Beaufighter being flown by Captain Dickson was hit, and in the terrible crash which followed, the pilot lost his life. Steve wrote, 'To us it was just another day's work. You couldn't allow yourself to think of what might happen … I was too busy to feel afraid during the actual attack.'

Decorated for Bravery

When Steve returned home after the war, his father and stepmother told him that they had prayed for his safety three times a day. In addition, they had read the words of Psalm 91 and were thankful that the promises of protection in the midst of danger described in that passage had been literally fulfilled in his case.

Shortly after this, a telegram arrived at his home. It read:

> 'Congratulations. You have been awarded the Distinguished Flying Cross. The South African Air Force is proud of you.'

George Stevens with his second wife, Margaret

Only a few men received this recognition. Steve was later to comment, 'In my opinion all the men deserved this award as much as we did.'

After the War

News of the dropping of the atomic bombs on Japan hit the headlines around this time. As the war finally came to an end, Steve, who was still an officer in the SAAF, asked himself the inevitable question. What next for me?

The answer was a short term task: to bring South African servicemen back home. Some had been prisoners. Some were wounded. The men were assembled at Cairo, and Steve, along with other pilots, flew Dakota transport aircraft backwards and forwards, between Cairo and Pretoria. Even with aircraft this was a five-day journey, including overnight stops.

In August 1947 he married Kay Mowat in South Africa. She was of Dutch extraction. Her first husband had died young from a brain tumour, and Steve gladly took on her three-year-old daughter, Merle. They were to have three children of their own, Pam, Coleen and Tim. The marriage lasted sixty-five years. He always regarded Kay as a real heroine without whom he would have achieved much less. She was always by his side with wise spiritual insights. A man with a self-declared impatient nature probably benefited greatly from regular prudent advice.

Waging War on the Tsetse Fly

Now the SAAF had another task for Steve, and one which involved some

Kay and Steve: a wedding photograph taken in Durban in 1947

dangerous flying. The dreaded tsetse fly was endemic in three game reserves of Zululand. The fly could kill cattle, and if a human was bitten, the victim would contract the disease widely known as 'sleeping sickness', which would mean a slow lingering death. Most of those affected were Zulus.

The SAAF used old twin-engine Anson aircraft to fight the tsetse fly. Six of these planes would take off at dawn and fly at treetop height to spray the areas designated with DDT, which was stored in a tank located in the cabin behind the pilot. Flying these old aircraft at low level was extremely dangerous. A mechanical failure in just one of the engines would cause a fatal crash. Sometimes flocks of large birds, such as vultures, disturbed by the noise of the engines, would fly in front of the aircraft.

Tsetse fly

Bird strikes could cause disastrous accidents. With hindsight he recognized that he was fortunate not to have developed serious health problems from the DDT.

By now Steve was thinking of leaving the SAAF and using his flying skills in the service of Mission Aviation Fellowship, but he persisted with this dangerous job for over a year in order to save up enough money to enable him to make that move. He had learned that MAF (UK) would not have resources to pay his expenses. He and his family would have to live on his savings.

The Berlin Airlift

One more task for the SAAF would also enable him to save more from his salary. He was sent to fly in the Berlin Airlift. Nowadays the Berlin Airlift has almost faded from memory, but in 1948–49 it was the headline news of the Cold War. Conquered Germany had been divided into two halves. West Germany was divided into zones occupied by the US, Britain and France. East Germany was ruled by the USSR under the dictator, Stalin. The capital of Germany, Berlin, was located deep in East Germany. By international agreement, the city was divided into two parts—the West under the control of Britain, America, and France, and the East controlled by the USSR.

The Dakota was the type of aircraft flown by Steve during the Berlin Airlift

The Cold War had become extremely serious, and could easily have led to more war, this time between the West and the USSR. Stalin wanted to force the Americans and the British out of West Berlin so he could take control of the whole city. To achieve this he closed all access to the city by land, leaving only air routes, over which he had no control. This attempt to seize the whole of Berlin for Soviet Russia was described by General Lucius Clay, the US officer in charge of the Allied response, as 'one of the most ruthless efforts in modern times to use mass starvation for political coercion'.

Using Dakota transport aircraft from which the seats had been removed, Steve flew from Lübeck in the British zone of West Germany to Gatow aerodrome in West Berlin and back again. He made a hundred of these flights. On the outward journey the plane would be full of coal or other supplies. On the return flight to Lübeck, it usually contained passengers. These were mostly people in danger of serious persecution from the Soviet Communist authorities.

When Stalin called off the blockade of Berlin in May 1949, one of the greatest feats in aviation history had ended in victory. About 700 transport aircraft had flown over 277,000 separate flights, airlifting millions of tons of supplies to save over two million Berliners from starvation and subjugation. Steve always rightly felt proud of his small contribution to the rescue of Berlin from the iron grip of Stalin's Communism.

Mission Aviation Fellowship

British MAF was set up by a group of former Second World War airmen.

The co-founder was a British aircraft engineer named Stuart King. He and his friends had done their planning. A survey of where aircraft could be most useful had been done in 1948. It was clear to the project's pioneers that many missionaries on the African continent lived very isolated lives. If any of them were to become ill, often the only way for them to obtain medical help would be for the sick person to be carried overland on a stretcher. Such a trek for aid could last a month or more. It was obvious that transport was a major problem. On the other hand, if an aeroplane were available, it would be possible for them to be flown to the nearest hospital or clinic in a matter of hours. Stuart King and his friends had chosen South Sudan as the place most in need of their help. They had even bought an old plane called a Rapide, which was made out of wood and fabric. But they needed a pilot to fly it.

Steve had been aware of the project for some time. He was particularly drawn to it because he recalled the way in which his own life had been revolutionized by contact with missionaries. By September 1950, after resigning his commission in the SAAF, he was ready to become British MAF's first operational pilot. His wife and family would follow him to South Sudan in due course and make their home there.

Steve wondered, and with good reason, how an old fabric-covered biplane would cope in South Sudan's climate. Also, it had no two-way radio. This meant that initial operations had to be done by booking the plane in advance, rather than summoning it to respond to an emergency. Nevertheless, primitive airstrips were hacked into existence in areas where aircraft had hitherto been unknown. The words 'God's Bird' in Arabic were painted on the nose of the plane.

On 10 November 1950 Steve flew the Rapide out of Khartoum Airport to look for Doro, a newly cut airstrip in South Sudan near the

Doro village in South Sudan consisted of many groups of huts like these

border with Ethiopia. For Stuart King, who accompanied him, a dream had come true. He had prepared for this moment for over four years. The landing on the primitive airstrip at Doro made the Rapide the first aircraft ever to land in this otherwise unreached part of Africa. The local Mabaan Africans clustered around looking at this strange machine with awe.

This photograph shows the reaction of the people on seeing an aircraft close up, possibly for the first time

After the landing and the greetings, Steve walked over to Doro graveyard where some adults and children lay buried. The thought came to him that if only MAF had reached South Sudan earlier, many of these people could have been flown to hospital in Khartoum, and their lives might have been saved.

Life in South Sudan

After only a few months of living in the deep south of Sudan, the Stevens family began to realize the hazards of the enterprise. Their first house was a round thatched hut built by an American missionary. One night early in 1951 when everybody was sound asleep, one of the Stevens' children suddenly shrieked out, 'They are biting me'. Everybody else woke with a start. An army of ants in a column of less than a foot (30cm) wide was marching through the home in their millions. The attraction was the food supply which Steve and Kay had bundled on the floor some time earlier. Jumping up, and using torches, the distraught family could see ominous-looking ants with pincers, plus large numbers of smaller sugar ants. Sadly, repellent had not been placed at the feet of the beds which were occupied by the two girls, Merle and Pam. The night invasion was eventually repelled. Next morning it looked as if an ant war had taken place. The floor was littered with ant carcasses. Life in Sudan was certainly capable of many surprises.

Only twenty-four hours later an Aladdin lamp was lit ready for the darkness of the night. The flame was turned down low, but not low enough. There was some overhanging tinder-dry thatch from the roof just above the flame. A tiny fire appeared in the thatch of the family's hut. Within seconds that small flame became a raging inferno. Steve, Kay and the children were safe. However, all their possessions were destroyed. This included clothes, supplies, passports, birth, marriage and yellow fever certificates. Some things were irreplaceable: wedding presents and a camera with precious photographs of early MAF operations. To his chagrin, Steve's treasured pilot's log book was lost. Next morning, he was heard to say, 'Well, I suppose there is no tidying up to do.'

Bob Swart was the designer and builder of the now ruined hut. Undeterred by setbacks, Bob wanted to visit an otherwise unreached territory where a tribe called the Murle lived out their isolated lives. On 16 April 1951 the first survey of this inaccessible area called Pochalla was attempted. An airstrip had been made ready for the Rapide, but it was short, and the return take-off was tense because they skimmed over the trees at the end of the 'runway' by only a few feet.

One of the reasons Steve took the calculated risk of this take-off was because he was keen to return to base as soon as possible. Bob's wife, Morrie, was due to give birth. Instead of booking Steve and the aircraft for a flight

*The difficulties of travel in South Sudan without aircraft are
illustrated by this image of a party using mules*

to Khartoum, she had asked Dr Mary Smith, based fifty-five miles away, to deliver the baby. It was arranged that when birth pains began to come, Stuart King and Steve would jump into the aircraft and fly off to fetch the doctor. Three days after visiting Pochalla, Morrie's pains started. With a headwind it took forty minutes to reach Nasir, but only thirty minutes for the return flight with Dr Mary. Chloe was born that night.

On 4 June 1951 the inevitable happened. In spite of all their care and precautions, one of the Rapide's wheels broke the sun-baked surface of a crude airstrip at Abaiyat and sank into soft mud. As it was moving slowly to take-off position the plane tipped up on its nose with the tail in the air. All the eight seats had safety belts, so nobody was hurt. The

Nobody was hurt when the Mission's Rapide tipped onto its nose. Note the primitive nature of the airstrip.

repairs, done by Stuart and Steve, took eighteen days. It was a warning about the risks of using airstrips hacked out of the wilderness by unskilled labour. The surface of these simple landing strips had no basic reinforcement, which would have made things much safer.

The problem was a lack of resources. As it was, MAF had a virtual staff vacuum at home. Somebody was needed to sort out the administration in Britain, so that there would be adequate support for the work beginning to expand in South Sudan. That support was about to be provided in an unexpected way.

One day, Steve was at Doro using an axe to chop down a palm tree growing at the end of the airstrip. He straightened up after bending, and the vision in his right eye was blurred. He had a detached retina. The treatment and eventual surgery which he underwent was not successful. A serious and unexpected dilemma faced MAF. In spite of much searching, no replacement pilot was available. Steve provided reassurances that his vision was adequate, and trial flights proved him to be right. The problem to be faced was that requests for the services of the first MAF aircraft were increasing. More and more airstrips were being created out of the jungle. They were lifelines to the outside world. Steve carried on the work until early 1953, until a suitable replacement pilot could come.

Home Director of MAF

Steve and Kay left South Sudan with mixed feelings. They had formed deep friendships in isolated circumstances. The people who relied on the aircraft were bonded together with them by challenges and adventures. If Steve intended to stay with MAF, he was the ideal person to take up the duties of Home Director. The parting with Sudan and the return to the land of his birth was a kind of bereavement for all concerned.

The work in the UK was totally different. No take-offs which just cleared the trees, no short airstrips instead of proper runways. In other words, no risky flying. Also, no watching out for snakes, ants, fierce bees and other unexpected dangers. His skills as a pilot had been well-used. Now he had to build up the infrastructure of support which was urgently required.

Newsletters were produced. Invitations to speak to potential supporters gradually increased. Stuart King had taken and edited some film of the work in South Sudan. With a small sixteen millimetre projector and a screen,

A family photograph taken in London during 1953. Steve and Kay are shown with their children. Left to right: Tim, Pam (behind the model plane), Coleen and Merle.

Steve spread the news about the MAF project. As the work became more widely known, Steve was approached by pilots enquiring about serving with MAF. Some had not really considered the sacrifice involved. Flying in a hostile climate, using poor airstrips, and dealing with

Steve and Kay in later years. He points to a drawing of the aircraft he once flew in South Sudan.

emergency situations was new to most men. The ones who were suitable were usually encouraged to gain more flying experience, extra needed licences and further theological qualifications. One applicant, Max Gove, was only fourteen years old when he came to see Steve asking to be an MAF pilot. His ambition became a reality—in time!

By 1970, after seventeen years as Home Director, Steve felt it was time for this chapter of his life to close. Kay agreed. He had done all he could. The MAF project had taken off and was well and truly off the ground.

Promoting Christian Values

While busily occupied with organizing MAF, it seemed to Steve that the floodgates of immorality of all sorts had been opened in the 'permissive sixties'. He supported the foundation of an organization called Festival of Light (FoL). With zeal he threw himself into public protests against the most salacious displays of immoral behaviour in the media, on stage and elsewhere.

One high point was in 1971 when about 35,000 concerned people gathered in Trafalgar Square, London. A manifesto was produced. All the speakers forcefully exposed blatant moral evils, but the long-term results were disappointing.

Steve could see what the future was likely to hold. For the next six years in Britain he worked for FoL, which is now transformed into CARE (Christian Action Research and Education). Seeking new challenges, Steve and Kay moved to Australia. He became Executive Director of FoL (Australia), a prominent community standards organization. As in Britain, this involved much public speaking, writing articles, television appearances, and radio and press interviews. They returned to Britain seven years later. It was now 1985. Although officially retired, Steve continued to oppose flagrant evil and corruption in society as opportunities presented themselves.

In his mid-nineties Steve wrote, 'I can look on the past with gratitude to God for his faithfulness and care throughout my long life'. As for the future he had the definite Christian confidence that he would go where there will be 'no more death, neither sorrow, nor crying, neither shall there be any more pain for the former things are passed away (Revelation 21:4).'

Steve died in June 2016 aged 96.

More Information on Steve Stevens

My many contacts with Steve Stevens provided the photographs and information for which I am very grateful.

Steve Stevens' rank, Lieutenant, relates to South African forces' designations, and has no connection with RAF ranks, such as Flight Lieutenant.

He has written three books of autobiography. These give very detailed information about his remarkable career:

1. *Beaufighter Over the Balkans* (ISBN 1-84415-487-4; 978-1-84415-487-6) was published in 2006.

2. *Early Wings Over Africa* (ISBN 978-1-905991-56-3) was self-published in 2010.

3. *Fighting for Love, Purity, Marriage and Family Life* (ISBN 978-1-905991-83-9) was published by New Wine in 2012.

The image of Steve's Beaufighter firing its rockets at Žužemberk on 13

February 1945 has appeared in other books, and on the Internet. Steve, however, owns the copyright and it was his very acceptable wish to use it for this book. To Steve, in his mid-nineties at the time of writing, it brings back vivid memories of dangerous missions while flying with 19 Squadron (SAAF).

Anybody studying the origins of British Mission Aviation Fellowship must read the official account called *Hope Has Wings* (ISBN 1–874367–58–2; 978–1–874367–58–1) by Stuart King, published by MAF (UK).

MAF's website shows a startling growth to a fleet of 130 aircraft operating in 30 countries. (Accessed 27/11/2013).

Jane Haining:
Scottish martyr

I t was May 1944. The D-Day landings in France were only a few weeks away. The Nazis were being driven slowly northwards in Italy. The Red Army was relentlessly pushing Hitler's forces from the east of Europe. The Germans were in full retreat on all the major battle fronts. At the same time in a corner of southern Poland a steam engine, pulling a long row of wagons, hissed its way slowly into some sidings. Nearby was the vast extermination camp of Auschwitz. From that dreaded place, enemies of the Nazis rarely escaped.

The line of drab cattle wagons behind the engine clanked to a halt. Guards dragged open the sliding doors, barking harsh orders to those inside. From the darkness of the foul-smelling interiors, pitiable victims of Nazi racism began to emerge. Out of one wagon a group of women were forced to jump down and to shuffle through the ominous gates towards their new home, the Auschwitz barracks.

A quick glance showed that all but one of the women in this column of human misery had a star on their clothing which identified them as Jewish. One, however, was markedly different in appearance. Unlike the Jewish ladies she had very fair skin, wore no star on her clothing, and the eyes behind her round-framed glasses were bright blue. Her name was Jane Haining, and she was a Scottish missionary who had been working among Jews in Budapest, the capital of Hungary.

How could she have ended up here? She was 1,300 miles from her peaceful home among the quiet rolling hills of Dumfriesshire in south-west Scotland. That must have seemed a whole world, indeed a whole lifetime, away.

Early Years

Jane Haining was born in 1897 at Lochenhead farm near the village of Dunscore, which had a population of about 150 people. It was nine miles (14 km) north-west of the town of Dumfries. To the south, Dumfriesshire borders the Solway Firth, from which the hills of Cumbria, in England, can be seen on a clear day. Her father, Thomas, was a farmer and the son of a farmer. Her mother, after whom she was named, died in childbirth in 1902 at the age of only thirty-six. Jane had two older sisters, Alison and Margaret. She also had a half-sister, Agnes, born in 1922, the daughter of Thomas Haining's second wife. Sadly, Thomas himself died in June 1922, only six months after his second marriage.

Lochenhead farmhouse as it looks today

The Haining family had a strong belief in God, and a lively Christian faith. They attended the nearby Craig Free Church of Scotland, not because it was customary to do so, but out of deeply held beliefs based on the Bible. Thomas was a deacon in the church at the time of the death of his first wife. Later, as a result of his spiritual qualities, he was appointed as an elder. His daughter Margaret subsequently recorded that faith in Christ as Lord and Saviour controlled the family attitudes, not only to church life, but to life in general.

Jane was baptized in the Presbyterian Free Church manner, and attended Sunday school as a young girl. She loved books, which gave her a clear grasp of the essential features of the Christian life. Indeed, Christ was always a living reality to her. Jane could never point to a specific time when she became a Christian. To her the date was unimportant. She had certainty of her salvation by Jesus Christ, and this was what mattered. She had no doubt that Christ had died for the sins of his people, including hers. Throughout her life, her words and deeds consistently demonstrated the sincerity of her personal faith.

Jane attended the local Dunscore village school until she was twelve. Both her class teacher and the headmaster, Mr Gold, recognized her intellectual gifts and encouraged her to take the examinations to qualify for a grant to attend Dumfries Academy, an old school with a fine, well-deserved reputation for good teaching and scholarship. As expected, Jane was

This photograph shows the original building of Dumfries Academy which Jane would have known during her education there from 1909 to 1915

awarded the grant to attend the academy. At the time a hostel for girls, the first of its type in Scotland, had just opened, and Jane Haining became one of its first boarders.

In 1915, when she was eighteen years old, she left the academy, having earned forty-one prizes and passing the Higher Grade examinations in English, Maths, Latin, French and German. The teachers were particularly impressed by her linguistic abilities. The First World War was now raging in Europe, so she returned to the farm to help out there. (Perhaps they were short-staffed because some of the men had volunteered to be soldiers). However, the family all knew that in the long run life on the farm would not be for Jane.

During the summer of that year Jane considered possible careers. She decided to work in the world of business. The Glasgow Athenaeum provided courses in commercial skills. She enrolled there and in 1917, when she had finished her studies, it was with the help of the Athenaeum's employment agency that she secured an appointment with J & P Coats Ltd., makers of all types of sewing thread. Now aged twenty, she started as a clerk, and in a short time obtained a well-paid post as a private secretary.

Her lodgings were deliberately chosen to be near her church. This was Queen's Park West Free Church in Glasgow. Here she had a rich and full life of friendship and service. Even though her work at J & P Coats was seven miles away in Paisley, she preferred to travel that distance to work every day so that she could more easily serve Christ in her local church. Soon Jane was put in charge of the whole Sunday school in this thriving church. One girl in her Sunday school class, Nan Potter, said of her, with typical childish exaggeration, 'There was nothing that she didn't know about the Bible.' She also recalled Jane taking them regularly to the City Bakery to buy them cream buns!

This comparatively modern reel of thread shows the name of Coats, the Paisley firm for which Jane worked

Near to Queen's Park Church was Renwick Congregational Mission. Jane helped regularly in the mission, showing that she had a serious concern for evangelism, even though she was by nature a very quiet character.

Interest in Foreign Missions

Margaret Coltart, Jane's cousin, was a missionary in India with a Canadian organization. The two women corresponded. Jane also set up a successful missionary library in her church. Her own interest in missions was growing. It was at this stage of her life that she felt the call to be a missionary, although she could as yet see no clear way how this could ever come about.

After the sudden death of Jane's father in 1922, the family farm was given up and Jane's stepmother returned home to her own family after her brief marriage. At the age of twenty-five Jane found herself bereft of both her father and the farm. Apart from links with her sisters, she now faced the world alone.

A Change in Direction

In 1927 Jane was with a friend when she heard an address by Rev. Dr George Mackenzie on missionary work among the Jews of Central and East Europe. She was so moved by the content of the lecture that she confided to the friend, 'I have found my life's work.' Now she knew that she wanted to work specifically in Jewish missions.

Jane began to read as much as she could about missions to Jewish people. She discovered that the Church of Scotland had a mission to Jews in Budapest. It was first established in 1841 and some very distinguished Jewish scholars had received Jesus Christ as Messiah as a result of its work. For instance, Jane learned that the well-known Scottish Hebrew scholar, John ('Rabbi') Duncan, had been an early missionary to Budapest. She was particularly interested to discover that a school and a home for girls were attached to the mission.

Her immediate superior at J & P Coats was Mr M. L. Peacock. She informed him of her decision to leave, but almost immediately he was unwell and had to be off work for five months. In his absence Jane was judged to be the only person who could carry on his work. Under some pressure she therefore stayed on until he returned. Then he appealed to her to stay longer until he had trained somebody to take her place. Again, she complied. Finally, she resigned, much to Peacock's dismay. Her employment at Coats had lasted over ten years.

To support herself until a door was opened for her to be a missionary, she withdrew her pension contributions. This amount, added to her savings, was all she had in the world.

The Divine Call

The habit of study was still with her and she enrolled at Glasgow School of Domestic Science where she studied for the Diploma and Housekeepers' Certificate. Still waiting patiently for divine guidance with regard to missionary service, she then took a temporary job as matron at the Paterson Institute in Manchester. A friend from Queen's Park Church continued to correspond with her. Every month this lady sent her a magazine published by the Church of Scotland called *Life and Work*.

Early in 1932 Jane was looking through a copy of this magazine when she saw an advertisement. There was a vacancy for a matron at the Girls' Home in Budapest. She applied, and in February of that year was offered the post. The salary was £100 a year. There was accommodation for her on the mission premises. Her excitement at the prospect of going to Budapest can only be imagined. It was an answer both to her patient waiting and to her prayers.

To Budapest

Preparation time was over. On 19 June 1932, nearly two weeks after her thirty-fifth birthday, a dedication service, conducted by Dr Stewart Thompson, Convener of the Jewish Mission Committee, was held in St Stephen's Church, Edinburgh, at which Jane was solemnly set apart for this particular Christian work. She wasted no time. The very next morning she set out for Budapest. The city is well known for being divided by the River Danube, with Buda on one side, and Pest on the other.

Jane was no stranger to life in a hostel for girls, having lived in one for six years while studying at Dumfries Academy. Almost at once she won the trust and affection of everybody in the mission. She liked them and they liked her. This was Jane's first close contact with Jewish people. Most, but not all of the girls in the hostel were Jewish. Many of the girls in Jane's care were sent to the home because they were not wanted. Easy divorce had led to the inevitable problem of the unwanted child. Orphans and abandoned children were numerous. Jane treated them all equally—kindly, but firmly when necessary.

The Church of Scotland had made a large financial investment in the mission building. By any standards it was impressive. It had five storeys, constructed around a rectangular courtyard. Living quarters and classrooms

The Church of Scotland Mission in Vorosmarty Street, Budapest, as it is today

were interlinked by open terraces. The Girls' Home was on the fourth floor. Not far away were the kitchen, dining room, a sewing room, a recreational area for games, dormitories, bathroom accommodation, a sick room and staff quarters.

Jane provides some information about the pupils in a report:

> There are about 400 pupils ranging in age from six to sixteen, and of these thirty to forty either live in or are day boarders ... we try to surround these girls with a Christian home atmosphere to instil into them by practice as well as precept what Christianity means. We have, for each class each day a Bible lesson when the Jewish children learn the New Testament.

With the help of the headmistress of the elementary school, Edit Roda, Jane became fluent in Hungarian by the end of 1933.

In 1935, after three years at the mission, Jane came home for a holiday, though she remained in Britain for only two months and gave no talks about her work. However, she visited the two-week-long Keswick Convention, held in the English Lake District. This was a time of serious Bible teaching, given to congregations of thousands. The speakers were able expositors of the Bible. The emphasis was on a growth in personal faith and holiness. Jane Haining's visit to Keswick in 1935 confirms that she was a Bible-believing Christian both by conviction and practice. The Bible was central to her personal faith. For Jane it was the inspired Word of God.

Nicholas Railton refers to a memory of Rev. Lajos Nagy, a Hungarian pastor at the mission where Jane worked. He recalls how she stopped at the main door of the mission before entering. She pointed to the hills of Buda and said, 'I always stop here before entering and say, "I lift up my eyes to the mountains, from whence cometh my help … my help cometh from the Lord."' (Psalm 121:1–2). This habit provides an illustration of her faith, which impinged on every aspect of her life.

Germany and Hungary during World War II

In January 1933 Hitler had become Chancellor of Germany and that country was rapidly engulfed in an avalanche of anti-Semitism. In 1940 the political leadership in Hungary decided to ally itself with Hitler against Britain. As a result the Hungarian Army took part in the German invasion of the USSR in 1941 and sent soldiers to fight the Red Army at the terrible Battle of Stalingrad in 1942. In 1944 Hungary opened negotiations with a view to changing sides and joining the Allies. Unfortunately for Hungary, the Germans found out. This action was seen as an impending betrayal. As a result, in March 1944 German forces occupied Hungary. Pre-arranged plans, largely organized by Adolf Eichmann, were put into action. Jews were steadily deported to Auschwitz. Though the Red Army was making progress in its steady push to the west, it would be January 1945 before the concentration camp at Auschwitz was liberated. By then an unknown number of Hungarian and refugee Jews, perhaps nearly 600,000, had been murdered at Auschwitz.

Jane's Response

Jane's personal response to anti-Semitism was to reassure the Jewish girls that she loved them. She commented, 'What a ghastly feeling it must be to know that no one wants you and to feel that your neighbours literally grudge you your daily bread!' A visitor wrote, 'She is a real mother to all the girls under her care.' Jane taught the girls that 'The greatest gift of the church to the Jews would always be Christ whom the Jewish Scriptures proclaimed.' The mission became a haven against anti-Semitism. Jane's first report to the Jewish Mission Committee in Scotland had spoken of the 'gradual influence of Christian care and teaching'.

Jane's hopes and prayers that God would use her 'to bring his people to a true knowledge of the saving love of Jesus' were in some measure answered. One example of this was the case of Marta Pauncz, née Szanto. She was one of the very few mission girls who survived the vicious treatment they received in a German concentration camp. Marta had first been taken under the wing of the mission in the 1920s. In 1946 she confided to Dr Alexander Nagy, a minister of the Hungarian Reformed Church, that 'her only help and saving comfort' had been her faith in Jesus Christ, who had been 'a living and constant companion' to her in the camp. She said, 'I am still unbaptized, but in heart and soul I am a happy follower of my Lord and Saviour Jesus Christ.' (Marta's actual letter is in the Church of Scotland Archive of the National Library of Scotland in Edinburgh).

Jane's final opportunity to go home was in 1939. She admitted to being exhausted by the demands of the work and was too fatigued, or else was simply reluctant, to give public talks about the work of the mission. However, she was accompanied on this brief visit to Britain by her friend, Margit Prém, the Hungarian headmistress of the High School, who was not only a Christian but also a fluent English speaker. Margit spoke at Aberdeen and Galashiels. Particularly moving was their visit to Jane's former church in Glasgow. Jane also squeezed in a visit to her sister Margaret, then living in Bromley, Kent. Their last week in Britain was spent relaxing in Devon and Cornwall. Jane's plan was to take her half-sister Agnes back to Budapest, but while they were in Cornwall the Second World War broke out in September 1939, and so the idea of taking Agnes to Budapest was abandoned.

There is a vivid record of Margit and Jane's nightmare journey back to the mission. They had to change trains five times. The carriages were packed as if it were a special holiday. There was no food, and no sanitation fit to mention. They even spent two nights sleeping on railway platforms on top of their own luggage. When they finally arrived at the mission, they found that everything was in confusion. On her return Jane worked flat out to restore order and as much normality as possible. By a titanic effort, she eventually restored as much smooth working at the mission as wartime conditions allowed.

A Crucial Decision

As the war became more threatening, with the fall of France in 1940 and the apparent dominance of German military power, the Church of Scotland instructed its mission workers to return home. Jane refused to leave her post. An urgent cable made no difference. She formally accepted the responsibility for her decision. Her biographer David McDougall states, 'Safety was not a matter that ever entered her mind.' With 315 pupils and 48 boarders, of whom, respectively, 224 and 31 were Jewish, Jane meant to stay where God had called her. One report states that she cut up her leather suitcases to make soles for the girls' shoes. One of her sisters, who probably knew her better than most, wrote, 'It was no surprise that she refused to come back when war was declared. After all, if the children needed her in peacetime, they had much more need of her in wartime, and she would never have had a moment's happiness if she had come home and left them ...'

Jane negotiated with Rev. Dr Louis Nagy for the Hungarian Reformed Church to take formal

The last photograph to be taken of Jane Haining (inaccurately called 'Mrs')

charge of the mission while the Church of Scotland was unable to do so. Ideally, she would have preferred to consult the church in Edinburgh, but communication was impossible.

Nearly four years of austerity and trouble followed. During this period her only link with home was the wireless, as the radio was called in those days. The calm and steady voices of BBC newsreaders gave her some modest comfort. Then came 19 March 1944, when the German army invaded Hungary. At once being Jewish became a serious problem. All Jews had to wear a yellow star. An observer saw Jane weeping as she sewed stars onto some of the girls' clothing

Arrest

On 4 April 1944 two men from the Gestapo, or secret police, searched Jane's office. They falsely claimed that they were looking for evidence that she was involved in espionage. She was given fifteen minutes to be ready to be taken away from the mission. She wanted to take her Bible, but it was tossed aside.

What had led to this sudden event? Piecing the evidence together, it is known that she had been denounced to the Gestapo by a member of Arrow Cross, the Hungarian Nazi Party. The man's name was Schréder and he was the son-in-law of the mission's housekeeper and cook, Mrs Kovács. Food for the youngsters was scarce, and when Jane discovered him eating food intended for the girls, she confronted him about it. This may well have led to his harbouring a personal grudge against her and a desire for revenge. His ideology, as a member of a Nazi party, would also have been a factor in the denunciation.

Initially Jane was held at Gestapo Headquarters in the Buda hills. After interrogation she was moved to Fő utca prison in the town. Her fellow prisoner was an English woman named Frances Lee. This lady had worked with the Church of England in Budapest for ten years, but not among the Jews. The two became friends. Frances spent eighteen and a half weeks in the cell, but unlike Jane was not sent to Auschwitz. While they were together, the two women would read a portion of Scripture every day before praying with each other.

The day Jane was taken from the cell she shared with Frances, the Gestapo officer made a sneering remark to Jane. He informed her that she would go to 'the Jewish Camp' since 'she loved the Jews so much'. After the war, Frances settled in New Zealand, from where she wrote a letter in which she records this comment and also lists the major charges made by the Gestapo against Jane. These were:

- That she had worked among the Jews.

- That she had wept when seeing girls wearing the yellow star.

- That she had listened to the BBC on the wireless.

- That she had visited British prisoners of war and taken them parcels.

- That she had been active in politics.

- That she had received English visitors.

- That she had dismissed her Aryan housekeeper.

In response to these charges, Jane pointed out that the law laid down that no Aryan could be employed where Jews lived. She also indicated that the Hungarian government had given her permission to visit the British prisoners of war and strongly denied that she was involved in politics. None of this helped her in the long run.

All attempts by the Swiss legation to rescue her from the clutches of the Gestapo were fruitless. The Swiss had given her a guarantee of safe

The gates leading into Auschwitz Concentration Camp. They carry the German words which translate as 'Work Makes Free'.

After her arrest Jane would have travelled to Auschwitz in a cattle wagon similar to this

conduct, but it counted for nothing. Her next destination after the time in Fő utca prison was Kistarcsa, about 15 miles (25 km). from Budapest. It was here that, on or about 12 May 1944, she was pushed into a foul cattle wagon with ninety women in it. In Auschwitz she was tattooed on her left forearm. Jane Haining was now Prisoner 79467.

There are several descriptions of the interior of the cattle wagons used to take victims to Auschwitz. Some Hungarian survivors have recorded the degrading conditions. The inmates were treated as if they were indeed cattle. For a gentle and loving woman like Jane, the dirt, smell, disease, death and disorder must have made it a virtually unbearable ordeal.

On 15 July 1944 Jane sent a postcard to Margit Prém. It was an official card headed Konzentrationslager Auschwitz and the instructions printed on it state that anyone who writes on the card must use only the German language and must write in pencil. In it Jane asks for food to be sent to the camp. All the evidence is that she was dying slowly of starvation. The main

These three official Nazi photographs show an unknown Jewish woman. Note the star and uniform worn by Jewish people.

part of the letter consists of questions about the state of the mission—which tells us that her heart was still in Budapest. Knowing that her words would be read by a censor, she ended, 'Here on the way to heaven are mountains, but they are not as beautiful or as high as ours.' Sadly, she must have known what was to come.

Two days later, on 17 July 1944, forty-seven-year-old Jane Haining was put to death, probably in a gas chamber. Cremation followed. She has no known grave. The letter she wrote is stamped with the date 21 July, by which time she was already in heaven. She had no more need of her precious Bible, which was eventually found in the rubble of the Girls' School. It contained a bookmark on which is written 'Be not afraid, only believe' (Mark 5:36).

Official news of her death came on 17 August. The German legation informed the Hungarian Minister of Foreign Affairs as follows: 'Miss Haining, who was arrested on justified suspicion of espionage against Germany, died in hospital of cachexia [severe constitutional weakness] following internal catarrh.'

On 22 August 1944 a Gestapo officer called at the mission with a bundle of her supposed personal effects. One of the papers in the bundle says that she died of 'natural causes'. Plainly all this was a pack of lies.

She was not the only Scottish person to die in a Nazi camp, as many accounts record. Probably about ten Scots died in this ghastly way. There are several memorials relating to Jane Haining in Scotland including a cairn in Dunscore paid for by public subscription and

Jane had been dead for over sixty years before local people erected a cairn in her memory

erected in 2005. In Budapest the main riverside road on the Pest side between the Chain and Elizabeth bridges once called Pest side lower embankment (Pesti alsó rakpart) has been renamed 'Jane Haining rakpart'.

A Letter from Anna

Some time after Jane's death a letter arrived at the mission. It was written simply in Hungarian by a girl called Anna. She records how her mother brought her to the school and how she found it strange and was reduced to tears. Suddenly she heard a pleasant voice: 'Oh, you would be our little Anna.' She could not see anything except Jane's blue eyes and she felt a motherly kiss on her cheek. 'So this was my first meeting with Miss Haining, and from this very moment I loved her with all my heart.' Through Jane's influence Anna's mother became a convert to Christianity. Mother and daughter presented themselves for baptism in the Reformed Church in Budapest, but the mother had no godmother for her daughter. In that awkward moment, Anna found Miss Haining standing by her side saying she was the godmother. The letter goes on with many compliments about Jane. Towards the end, it says:

> The days of horror were coming and Miss Haining protested against those who wanted to distinguish between the child of one race and the child of another. She recognized only the children of Jesus Christ. I still feel the tears in my eyes, and hear in my ears the siren of the Gestapo car. I see the smile on her face while she said 'Good bye' … I will never forget Miss Haining, and I will try to follow in her footsteps.

Righteous among the Nations

In 1988 Charles Walker, of the organization Scots Abroad, wrote a letter to Yad Vashem, the Holocaust martyrs and heroes remembrance authority in Israel. Walker asked whether Jane Haining qualified for the title 'Righteous Among the Nations' (the Israeli way of recognizing Holocaust heroes who suffered as a result of helping Jewish people). Yad Vashem made it clear that Jane was obviously involved in missionary work in Budapest. 'Surely,' said the reply, 'you do not expect a Jewish institute to award her for *this*?' Nobody is completely clear as to the reason why the committee of Yad

Vashem subsequently changed its mind, but in 1997, one hundred years after Jane's birth, the Church of Scotland received a letter informing it that 'the late Jane Haining, who suffered a martyr's death at Auschwitz for help to Jews in Hungary', had been awarded the title of 'Righteous Among the Nations'. That decision has led to a division of opinion among Scottish Jews. The 1997 decision to award her this status is now the official position of Yad Vashem, but there are still those in Scottish Jewry who think that the 1988 perspective is the correct one.

Jane Haining is far above such controversy. Her story of service and sacrifice, epitomized in the letter from Anna, speaks for itself. Her last letter tells us that she knew her ultimate destination. It was not Auschwitz; it was the glory of heaven.

More Information on Jane Haining

The first biography with any real credibility is by Rev. David McDougall. It is a forty-page booklet with the title *Jane Haining 1897-1944*. It was printed in 1949 by the Church of Scotland World Mission and reprinted in 1953, 1973 and 1988. Ian Alexander edited and updated the material in 1998. (There appears to be no ISBN).

In 2007 Dr Nicholas Railton wrote a well-researched book subsidized by the Church of Scotland, called *Jane Haining and the Work of the Scottish Mission with Hungarian Jews, 1932-1945* (ISBN 978-963-7893-32-2). It is bilingual, with the text printed in both English and Hungarian.

Other sources, particularly ones that appear on the Internet, often contain inaccuracies, and should be compared with the two sources quoted above, on which this chapter is based.

No high-quality images of Jane Haining appear to have survived. The picture of her used in this account was supplied by the Church of Scotland offices.

The reel of thread showing Coats' name came from Hazel Stephens' old sewing basket and was photographed by David Poll.

Rev. and Mrs David White kindly travelled to Dunscore at my request in April 2015 and took the photographs of Lochenhead farmhouse and the other scenes in Dunscore as they appeared at that time.

The photographs of the Auschwitz gates with their untrue wording ARBEIT MACHT FREI, and the three-position official Nazi photograph of a Jewish lady, derive from the Auschwitz-Birkenau State Museum in Oświęcim, Poland, and are used with official permission.

www.auschwitz.org is relevant to this story.

From Matron to Martyr by Lynley Smith is an attempt to fictionalize Jane Haining's story as if she kept a diary. If anybody reads this book they need to be reminded that it is fiction, and is therefore not to be relied on as a source. It was published in the USA by Tate Publishing in 2012. It has 208 pages. ISBN 978–1–61862–200–6.

The Scottish Christian Mission building was heavily damaged towards the end of the Second World War. It has been rebuilt as Vorosmarty School, and may be found in Vorosmarty utca (street), 51, in the centre of Budapest.

3

Jim Glazebrook: U-boat hunter

'The only thing that really frightened me during the war was the U-boat peril.'

So wrote Winston Churchill in his six-volume history of the Second World War. Almost all historians agree that probably the most dangerous weapon which the Nazis used against Britain in that terrible war was the U-boat. These German submarines sank a large number of Allied ships, causing numerous casualties among seamen and huge losses of supplies. Indeed, had they been reinforced, they would have had the potential to starve Britain into submission.

One important aspect of the Allied response to the menace posed by the Nazi submarines involved the aircraft of RAF Coastal Command. Many brave airmen from this organization perished in the unforgiving sea while flying anti-submarine patrols. Flight Lieutenant J. J. V. Glazebrook DFC, known to his friends as Jim, took the same risks as the men who were lost, but survived to see the peace—and write a memoir. This is his story.

Family and Schooling

Jim Glazebrook was born in 1920 in Teddington, Middlesex, England. His early life was dominated by the repercussions of his parents' separation in 1927. From then on, Jim lived with his father at Wallington in Surrey, while his sister, Marietta, lived elsewhere with his mother. At the age of ten

Jim left Wallington Primary School and, having passed the appropriate entrance examination, was admitted to Christ's Hospital School near Horsham, in Sussex.

Important decisions about Jim's future were influenced by his father's experience of unemployment in the Great Depression of the 1930s. When RAF officers visited Jim's school on a recruiting drive, he would have liked to apply for a Short Service Commission. His father, however, thought otherwise. He believed that such a route was a dead end. As a result, Jim was persuaded to join the

Jim, aged 8, at Wallington

Post Office Telephone Service. His father deemed this to be a safe career, with an established promotion structure and a good pension. In normal circumstances Jim would have stayed on at school until he was nineteen, but the Post Office insisted that they would prefer him to have three years' experience with them, rather than remain at school studying for examinations not related to the Telephone Service. As a result Jim left school mid-term in 1936 and became an engineering apprentice. This effectively put paid to any possibility of his going to university.

Spiritual Influences

The Royal Charter of Christ's Hospital School, dated 1553, describes it as a 'Religious, Royal and Ancient Foundation'. Along with all the boys he knew, Jim accepted that a service would be held in the school chapel every morning. 'I do not recall ever being challenged in a personal way,' he wrote later. By his own account, the rituals observed in chapel induced daydreaming. Those who led the school services went through a routine of exhortations to be 'good and religious', without any reference to the fact that the Christian faith involves a personal relationship with Jesus Christ. The 'religious' teaching consistently omitted the truth that at the centre of the

Christian faith stands a cross, and on that cross there is the crucified figure of the Son of God, whose sacrificial death cleanses those who believe in him from all sin. The biblical perspective of the centrality of the cross and the resurrection, which is always life-changing, was missing from these services.

Jim first heard the real Christian message in 1934, when he was fourteen. He heard it from two sources. First, with his father's encouragement, he attended the Christian Union at Christ's Hospital. This met weekly, and speakers were invited who explained the biblical message clearly. Many of these were former students of Christ's Hospital School, known as 'Old Blues'. Secondly, Jim also attended Wallington Crusader Bible Class, along with over 200 other boys. The need to receive Jesus Christ as personal Saviour was emphasized in these classes. He records, 'I do not recall any gospel appeal to which I did not respond with my heart, yet there was no dramatic moment of decision as such. I have never doubted the existence of God and have always wanted to serve him.'

Jim's life of faith may have begun in 1934, but it took some time for him to mature into a believer with a vibrant spiritual life, an admirable sacrificial lifestyle and a coherent understanding of the biblical message. By 1938, however, he was one of the leaders of the Wallington Bible Class, fully competent to teach the Bible to other young men.

Training to be a Pilot

In the late 1930s the prospect of war was seen as a serious possibility by most people in Britain. In that event the danger that London would be bombed was very real. With this in mind, most of the big banks and insurance companies which were based in London made contingency plans to move to large country houses in the rural areas surrounding the capital. Jim was involved in the installation of telephone switchboards in many of these buildings.

On Sunday, 3 September 1939, the expected happened. Britain was once again at war. Bombing raids on London started in 1940. In the bright, sunny summer of that year, many folk living in the south-east of England could observe the Battle of Britain taking place in the skies over their heads.

Jim was one of them. As he saw the RAF fighters desperately resisting the German planes, his desire to join in the struggle grew. Although the RAF was successful in that crucial battle, it lost many airmen and an appeal went out for men to train as pilots or navigators. Early in 1941 four men from the same telephone exchange were all given permission to volunteer. They enrolled on the same day. Jim wrote, 'All of us became pilots. The other three failed to return from operations.'

Today Elmdon airfield is known as Birmingham International Airport. In 1941 it was the place where the RAF taught Jim to fly. On 18 November 1941, after tuition lasting six-and-a-quarter hours, Jim went solo. He wrote, 'I flew round the circuit in my open cockpit biplane banging the outside of the aircraft and singing, "Praise my soul the King of Heaven" at the top of my voice.' Jim always felt sad that his father, who died unexpectedly in 1940 at the age of forty-three, did not live to see him become a pilot.

The next part of his training took part in the United States. He was sent to a huge US Navy airbase at Pensacola in Florida. Jim proved to be an exceptionally competent pilot. He flew a succession of US aircraft, including Catalina flying boats. On 25 November 1942 he was awarded the official US Navy's airmen's certificate. Having asked permission to join the armed forces some two years earlier, he was by now seriously wondering if he would ever take part in the war in Europe.

Miss Kathlyn Monroe (Aunt Katie) June 1942

'Aunt Katie'

During Jim's time at Pensacola, he and other Christians he met attended services at First Presbyterian Church. The genial Scottish minister, Dr Thomas, was happy that many of his congregation invited the British visitors to meals in their houses. Kathlyn Monroe was a schoolteacher who was in charge of the young people's work in the church. She collected

United States Naval Air Station

Pensacola, Florida

Know all men by these presents that

Sergeant Pilot John B. Glazebrook, Royal Air Force

has completed the course of training and has met successfully the requirements of the course as prescribed for

Naval Aviators of the United States Navy

In Witness Whereof, *this certificate has been signed on this* 25th *day of* November 19 42 *and the Seal of the Naval Air Station hereunto affixed*

Commander, U. S. Navy
Superintendent of Aviation Training

Captain, U. S. Navy
Commandant, Naval Air Training Center

US Navy pilot's qualification certificate, November 1942

details about the young British visitors, ostensibly so that she could write to their families if anything unpleasant happened. The young men called her 'Aunt Katie'. They did not take long to discover that she wrote letters to all their families back at home reassuring them that their young men were in

While at Pensacola Jim proved to be an exceptional pilot, even learning to fly Catalina flying boats like this one

good health and behaving themselves very well. They enjoyed her food and her kindness.

When Jim's course ended in November 1942, none of the British airmen knew where they would be spending the coming Christmas. Aunt Katie put that right. She laid on a slap-up Christmas dinner with ingredients that could only be dreamed of in a Britain afflicted by severe rationing.

Aunt Katie with some Christian guests. Jim is on the far left

Thirty years later she would make her one and only trip outside America, to visit these men. She had always cherished an ambition to go to the UK 'to see my boys', as she called the young servicemen she had befriended. Jim was one of those she visited. He took her to see the English Lake District. Aunt Katie, servant of God, died in 1979 aged eighty-three, and her 'boys' promptly had a memorial plaque to her put up in the Pensacola Presbyterian Church.

The Azores

Jim was not yet finished with training. From Pensacola he was sent to the Bahamas, where he made friends with John Johnston, another Christian believer. The minister of the Methodist Church in Nassau had been a missionary, and his sermons about Christ provided the two young men with the spiritual food they needed. The invitation which they received to have dinner with the Duke and Duchess of Windsor was ultimately not nearly as important as meeting that elderly minister. (The Duke was the former King Edward VIII of Britain, who had abdicated in December 1936, and became Governor of the Bahamas during the war years).

John and Jim dressed smartly ready to meet the Duke and Duchess of Windsor

Since Jim was a qualified captain of a Liberator bomber, he was surprised to be posted to a squadron flying, not Liberators, but Fortresses. These planes were based on Terceira, one of the Azores islands owned by the Portuguese, and situated 900 miles (1,450 km) west of Portugal in the Atlantic Ocean. From Lagens, the local airfield (now called Lajes) the Allies could fly north to the centre of the vast ocean. As a result U-boats came within range of Allied aircraft. For the rest of the war Jim served with 206 Squadron on anti-submarine patrols and operations. His description of the conditions under which they worked is vivid:

> Searching for U-boats involved long weary hours of flying over the sea, twelve-and-a-half hours being the standard patrol time for the Fortress. Often we had nothing to show for it. All the crew had seen was endless sea. Such

patrols however, were not wasted. The submarines at that time could not travel very far or at any speed under water. So, if the presence of a patrolling aircraft kept them submerged they were prevented from getting to where they might do their deadly work.

When a U-boat was spotted, we had to act quickly. We carried depth charges, not bombs. These are explosive devices specially designed for underwater use. They had to be dropped from only fifty feet (15 metres) above the water. My normal patrol height was 800 feet (244 metres). In a crash dive a U-boat could be out of range of our depth charges in seconds.

More unpleasantly, instead of diving, a U-boat might stay on the surface to fight. This happened more and more towards the end of the war. Cannons fitted in the sub's conning tower could put up a frightening barrage to an aircraft approaching at only fifty feet. One serious hit on an attacking aircraft would almost certainly cause it to crash into the ocean with the loss of all aboard. Many aircraft were shot down in this way before having a chance to drop their depth charges. This happened to one of our flight commanders in January 1944 while flying from the Azores. When we were faced with a surfaced U-boat a few weeks later you may well imagine our feelings …

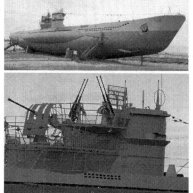

This preserved U-boat, U-995, shows the cannons fitted on the conning tower with the aim of shooting down RAF aircraft, and so feared by pilots like Jim Glazebrook

It was the night of 12–13 March 1944 … my Fortress was sent to where U-575 had been attacked by another RAF plane. As it grew light I circled

Fortress of 206 Squadron taken immediately after landing following the attack on U-575. The crew, including Jim, is clustered by the aircraft.

the Fortress around the spot where U-575 had submerged. While gazing at the seemingly endless ocean, I suddenly saw the same U-boat surface. Perhaps the captain thought he could shoot down the Fortress if it attacked. All the sub's cannons were fully manned. The crew of the Fortress made a unanimous decision to attack. We dived down to fifty feet above the waves. In an attempt to upset the aim of the gunners, we corkscrewed our approach to the submarine. Four depth charges exploded around the U-boat. It vanished below the waves. But had we sunk it? We circled the spot for five hours until lack of fuel made us return to the Azores.

The damaged U-575 was finally destroyed by other aircraft and ships. On landing at Lagens, the first words of a member of the crew who told everybody he was an atheist were: 'You were not the only one praying, Jim.' The simple truth was that they were all fortunate to survive the action against U-575.

Operation Cork

Two weeks later Jim was posted back to the UK. He flew his Fortress to an airfield in Norfolk where it was left for use by others. His friend John Johnston

Jim (centre of back row) as pilot of a Liberator with his crew at Leuchars, Scotland, in August 1944

joined him on a train from Norfolk to London. Between them, they had so much luggage that it had to be left in the corridor of the railway coach. Included in this luggage was a large bunch of bananas, a fruit unknown in England in 1944. After five minutes they noticed that about twenty bananas had vanished. Jim finishes the story: 'Thereupon John and I decided that if others were to have our bananas we would decide who should receive them. So we walked the length of the train and gave a banana to every child. Most did not know what they were, but their mothers were delighted!'

By June 1944 the Allied invasion of mainland Europe was all set to go. Thousands of invasion craft had to cross from England to the Normandy coast. It was essential that the shipping should be protected from the U-boats. Jim was sent to an airfield in Cornwall, called St Eval. Crowded onto this airfield, over thirty Liberator aircraft were ready to block the English Channel to U-boats. All flew to a strict timetable day and night, with one plane following another at thirty-minute intervals. As a result, the U-boats were unable to hinder the invasion of Europe. Operation Cork, aptly named, was a success. So was D-Day.

Flying from Scotland

For the remainder of the war Jim pursued the U-boats in northern waters. The winter of 1944–45 was noted for atrocious weather. Half of the losses incurred by Jim's unit were a direct result of the ineffective weather-forecasting of the time. Jim illustrates this from experience.

On one occasion he took off at 4.00 a.m. from his Scottish base at Leuchars. As he flew west, over the seemingly limitless ocean, the weather, which had been bad at take-off, became worse. As captain of the Liberator, he carried the responsibility of the lives of his crew of nine. That meant there were ten lives to consider, including his own.

A Liberator of 206 Squadron, Coastal Command. This is the aircraft flown by Jim while based in Scotland.

If he pressed on in deteriorating weather conditions and they ditched in the sea, none of them would survive more than five minutes. Nobody would have blamed him if he had turned back. On the other hand, they had been told that there was a convoy ahead waiting for protection. If he turned back and a U-boat sank one or more of the ships, the loss of life would be far greater than that of a single aircrew.

Jim recorded his thoughts:

> So what did I do? The psalmist wrote, 'In my distress I called upon the Lord and he heard my voice.' Well I did just that. I cried from my heart, 'Lord, what ought I to do?' Most unusually … I was given an immediate answer. I heard a voice, no not really a voice, though the words came into my head every bit as clearly as if a voice had spoken. I heard the words from a psalm written by King David about three thousand years ago. How in the world could God and the Bible help my situation? Listen.

> 'If I take the wings of the morning and remain in the uttermost parts of the sea even there shall thy hand lead me and thy right hand shall hold me' (Psalm 139:13).

> 'The wings of the morning-in the uttermost parts of the sea.' It took my breath away. It could not have been more up to date if King David had been a pilot. Anyway, I knew I was being told that we would complete our mission safely. We flew through the sleet and over the dirty grey sea below us—and returned safely.

> Now the moral of the story is, 'Do not believe the fallacy that the Bible is out of date.' If it can meet the need of a young and frightened pilot over the Atlantic in the 1940s, it can meet anyone's need today … it is the living Word of God.

Since becoming a Christian, Jim was convinced that the Holy Spirit speaks through Scripture, making its message alive to believing readers.

Foula

Every man who flew in the RAF was required to keep a log book. This recorded all the flights the airman made, noting not only the dates but also any action taken by, or against, the enemy. Jim flew nearly 2,000 hours in RAF aircraft. Reading the record of his consistent bravery and the way he, and men like him, faced hazards makes jaw-dropping reading. The strain of constantly patrolling over the cruel sea while flying at deliberately low altitudes must have been immense.

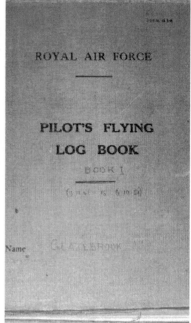

The logbook contains a record of every flight Jim made while serving in the RAF

On one occasion, when he was approaching his twenty-fifth birthday, Jim did give up the fight against the weather. His allotted patrol area was between the Shetlands and the Faroe Islands, which are halfway between Norway and Iceland. This covered a route used by the Germans to get their submarines into the Atlantic. It was night. The aircraft was encrusted with ice. The weather deteriorated more and more. The navigator had little idea where they were. The island of Foula is twenty miles (32 km) west of the Shetlands. It remains one of Britain's most remote inhabited possessions with well under fifty inhabitants. Foula has sheer sea cliffs which rise to 1,300 feet (396 metres). Flying almost 'blind' at 250 feet (76 metres) above the sea, Jim missed the unforgiving cliff by an uncomfortably close margin. Afterwards the crew realized just how close they had been to a violent death. Those who live without God in their lives call this kind of thing 'luck' or 'fate'. Jim called it an answer to prayer. By prayer he had become a Christian; by prayer he lived as a Christian.

The Final Surrender of the U-Boats

Jim's squadron was constantly in action and regularly suffered losses until the surrender of Germany in May 1945. In February of that final year of the war, Coastal Command made a big attack on the U-boat training grounds in the Baltic Sea. Fourteen planes were involved. They flew all the way to the Baltic at or below 200 feet (61 metres). After this very dangerous operation Jim was awarded the Distinguished Flying Cross (DFC). The award was not just for this action in the Baltic, but for consistent bravery in action since he had started flying against the U-boats.

Awards for bravery are printed in *The London Gazette*, the British official public record published since 1665. The issue dated 6 April 1945 contained the following entry:

RAF AWARDS ... DFC

Pilot Officer J. J. V. Glazebrook, 206 Squadron

One night recently this officer was pilot and captain of an aircraft detailed for a sortie. Whilst over the Baltic he engaged an enemy merchant vessel and pressed home a good attack at low level. Shortly afterwards he went into the attack against a force of five U-boats, escorted by a surface naval vessel ... Although he had lost the element of surprise, Pilot Officer Glazebrook returned to the attack. In spite of considerable anti-aircraft fire from all the vessels, this resolute pilot released his depth charges on one of the U-boats. He showed coolness, courage and determination of a high order.

When the war ended, over 200 U-boats were still at sea. Jim saw many of them surrender, and even went on board one that had been captured. The submarine captain boasted that he could remain submerged for eighty-one days. Jim could think of nothing worse than being cooped up for any length of time in what he thought of as little more than an elaborate metal tube. He asked his enemy if this was a strain. The retort was: 'No, the longer we remained submerged, the less likely we are to be attacked by aircraft.' 'So,' thought Jim, 'they really did fear our aircraft.'

Peacetime

In September 1946 Jim was released from regular RAF service. He was twenty-six. There were several employment possibilities open to him. He could apply to be a permanent officer in the RAF, or he could become an airline pilot. He was more interested in joining the British branch of Mission Aviation Fellowship (MAF), an organization which at this stage had scarcely got off the ground. The idea of using aircraft to save lives, instead of destroying them, appealed to Jim. However, pilots who hoped to work for MAF needed to be fully qualified aircraft engineers and also to have some ability with foreign languages, as they would be flying in remote places, probably in parts of Africa where English was not widely spoken. Jim

Jim and Betty were married at Glenarm, Northern Ireland, 1 June 1950

was a first-class pilot, but he was not an engineer. Nor did he have any foreign-language skills. In the event, Jack Hemmings, who had been at Christ's Hospital School with Jim, was to fly MAF (UK)'s first plane.

Neither of the other options appealed to Jim as a permanent career and so, with no strong leanings to do anything else, he resumed his former employment. The Post Office Telephone Service had kept his job open for him, so he rejoined them—though with a higher position.

Two years before this, in 1944, Jim and his crew had been sent on a short-term posting to Northern Ireland. His friend John Johnston was elated, as his family home at Glenarm was very near to the airbase. While they were there, the whole crew was invited to a meal at John's parents' house. Also present on this occasion were two young sisters. Six years later Jim was to marry one of them, Betty Crawford!

The marriage took place in the Presbyterian Church in Glenarm in June 1950. Jim and Betty's first house was at Wallington in Surrey. Both joined the parish church nearby, where Jim had confessed his faith in confirmation. It was a happy marriage and they were both assets to the church in different ways.

Jim's career in the Post Office advanced as time went by. In 1957 he moved to a more senior post in Manchester. From 1975 he was in charge of the whole telephone service in the north-west of England. This covered a large area including the Lake District. Though his office was in Lancaster, he and Betty made their home at Burton-in-Lonsdale. (It was here that Aunt Katie visited them). The nearby parish church, which they attended, was Bible-based.

Retirement came in 1981. On his last day at work, the telephone service was separated from the Post Office, and became British Telecom, now known as BT.

Even in the years of peace Jim still retained the desire to fly as a pilot. Wherever he was living, he nearly always joined the local civilian flying club. He was also a pilot with the RAF Reserve until it was closed down in 1953. During this period he was recommissioned as a Flying Officer. Jim now gave Experience Flights to two University Air Squadrons based at Woodvale, near Southport, Lancashire. As a Flight Lieutenant he made his final official flight in charge of an RAF aircraft in March 1965.

Far more important to him was helping Mission Aviation Fellowship. He was the first Area Representative to serve MAF as a volunteer in the north-west of England. Over the years he gave over 400 presentations about the work of MAF to schools, church organizations and, indeed, any group who would listen. In this way MAF became better known.

The Church of England licensed him to take services, and he often did so in churches which were without a minister, or where the regular minister was ill. For many years he also took Remembrance Services. Adding all these services together, he preached several hundred times.

Expressing his Christian Faith

The driving force in the life of Jim Glazebrook was plainly his Christian faith. In 2008 he wrote a Christmas letter to over 300 distant friends. In it he included a commendation of a book he had just re-read. It was Liam Goligher's book *The Jesus Gospel*. He wrote:

> It reminded me of the need to persuade people that Christ is the only Saviour of the world, that hell is as real as heaven, and that people must trust Christ alone for salvation. Liam Goligher quotes the apostle Paul, 'We implore you on behalf of Christ to be reconciled to God' (2 Corinthians 5:20). Eternal issues are at stake and … it is imperative that you make the right choice.

During Jim's later years, when they were living in a flat in Knutsford, Cheshire, I made as many visits to see him and Betty as possible—as well as regular telephone calls. As Christmas 2010 approached, Jim questioned whether he had the physical stamina to carry on producing about 300 copies of the Glazebrooks' seasonal newsletter without help. I suggested that he should use the 2010 letter to quote some of his favourite Bible verses. He wrote in the letter:

> The best-known verse in the Bible fulfils a promise from God. It says, 'For God so loved the world, that he gave his only begotten Son, that whosoever believeth in him should not perish, but have eternal life' (John 3:16).

> The next verse continues, 'For God sent not his Son into the world to condemn the world; but that the world through him might be saved.'

> He [Jesus] also said, 'I am the way, the truth, and the life; no man cometh unto the Father, but by me' (John 14:6).

> And Peter said of Jesus, 'Neither is there salvation in any other; for there is

none other name under heaven given among men, whereby we must be saved' (Acts 4:12).

At the end of his letter Jim concludes, 'I pray that these great truths may be (or will become) as real to you as they are to me.'

An Unexpected Trauma

Jim's faith had been put to a severe test in 1996. Having no family of their own, he and Betty decided to go on a world tour to visit as many of their relatives and friends as possible. Both had lived full lives and they had made a point of maintaining contact with many friends. They were in Napier, New Zealand, visiting some of Betty's family, when she suffered a stroke with very severe mental and physical consequences. Jim's dynamic wife was now reduced to almost total disability. Until her death in 2012, Jim treated her with sacrificial love and endless patience. He served her in

Betty and Jim in old age

all the small, unnoticed ways required by a disabled person. When she died he remarked, 'She has gone home.' The two words 'gone home' expressed his sense of victory over the last enemy—death.

The citation for Jim's DFC said that when he faced the enemy in the most dangerous circumstances, 'he showed coolness, courage and determination of a high order'. Those who had the privilege of knowing Jim personally saw another side of him. On the surface he was humble, very quiet and self-effacing, a classic example of an ordinary man with extraordinary achievements. In the foreword to Jim's memoir, *Someone to Watch over Me*, the head of British MAF summed him up like this:

I see in Jim many of the qualities we see in Barnabas. He, too, was a man deeply committed to the cause of Christ, never counting the cost of following the Master, but always with one eye on the personal needs of others. Always prepared to offer the hand of friendship to those with whom he came into contact.

Jim Glazebrook died in 2014, aged ninety-four. It was a long life, a full life and, more importantly, a life well lived for the Lord. He has now taken the wings of the morning and found that God's hand does indeed hold him.

More Information on Jim Glazebrook

Jim's Memoir *Someone to Watch over Me* was published by RoperPenberthy Publishing Ltd, Horsham, England in 2005 (ISBN 1–903905–23–0; 978–1–903905–23–4).

The illustrations were almost entirely supplied by Jim Glazebrook.

Thain Flowers supplied the image of Jim and Betty in their later years.

John Lowe supplied the photograph of Jim's pilot's log book. John has created a fine Internet site devoted to the history of 206 Squadron. This was the unit in Coastal Command to which Jim was assigned and with which he did most of his flying.

Readers should consult: www.coastalcommand206.com

Some readers will notice that the initial in Jim Glazebrook's name is written wrongly on his US Navy pilot's qualification. It should say John J.V. Glazebrook.

Bastiaan Ader:
Dutch resistance leader

In 1949 Queen Wilhelmina of the Netherlands officially opened the Loenen Field of Honour. In this serene and secluded place of seventeen hectares (forty-two acres) are nearly 4,000 graves of Dutch victims of war, particularly the Second World War. The Netherlands War Graves Foundation cares for the beautiful tree-lined site. Every grave is simple in design. The fascinating stories behind every interment are carefully recorded. There is none more remarkable and worthy of recording than that of Bastiaan Ader, the subject of the following account.

Bastiaan Jan Ader, or Bas as he was usually called, was named after his father, who was the head teacher of an elementary school. He was born at 's-Gravenzande, a small town in South Holland, on 30 December 1909. During his childhood, he and his sister Gepke were often moved from place to place. After leaving primary school, Bas attended a secondary school in Wageningen, although he was living in Ede. He was always interested in railways, and that certainly would have fuelled his early ambition to be a railway engineer.

He was part of a united, loving family, all of whom were committed to the Dutch Reformed Church. This was more than just a formality; it was a matter of sincerely held belief in the Christian gospel. For them, being a Christian meant having a personal relationship with the living Christ, something that was expressed in prayer and study of the Bible as well as in public worship. Bas made a personal commitment to Jesus as Lord during a time of inner struggle. Later, he became conscious of a divine calling to be a minister. As a result, he transferred to a grammar school in Deventer, where the curriculum included the subjects he would need to study in order to qualify for university entrance.

Bas was a gifted musician and was not only successful in passing the examinations that formed part of the school curriculum, but also those needed for the post of official organist at a church in Lochem, a small city in the eastern Netherlands. He even carried out restoration work on the organ at Lochem, adding fourteen new 'voices' to its range, thereby increasing its usefulness. All through his life, he also composed music, having found inspiration in the musical work of César Franck (1822–90). Sadly, the only one of Bas's compositions that still survives today is a Christmas cantata.

Love and Marriage

Johanna Adriana Appels, the daughter of a very well-to-do family from Utrecht, was sitting alone in an otherwise empty compartment of a train when a young man, at least six feet tall, with blonde, wavy hair, came in and sat down. He noticed the copy of a history book by Rijpma lying on her lap and they began to talk. Before long it became clear that they were both students at Utrecht University. She was studying English, and sang in a choir. More importantly, they discovered that they each shared the same faith in God. They parted without sharing addresses and

Jo Ader

Jo, as everybody called her, wondered if she would ever see this interesting young man again. (The fact that he was reading theology made him even more attractive to her). Some time later, however, they unexpectedly caught sight of each other in Utrecht's Wilhelmina Park. She ran towards him, losing her bonnet as she did so!

On 25 September 1935 Bas and Jo were married in the Dutch Reformed Church of William the Silent (known as the 'Father of our Fatherland') in Amsterdam. It was customary to include a 'wedding psalm' in the service. Nobody knows who chose it, but on this occasion the psalm was Psalm 27.

Bas and Jo. A wedding photograph from 1935

Round about this time, Bas wrote a long poem, addressed to Jo, based on the old Graeco-Roman legend told by Ovid about Baucis and Philemon, whose greatest wish was that they should die together.

Bas and Jo made their home in a flat overlooking the Leiden Canal in Amsterdam. All the furniture was designed and handmade with some considerable skill by Bas. One evening as they walked together towards the setting sun alongside one of the canals, he remarked, 'I think that a very eventful life awaits us.' It was almost as though he had a premonition of what the future would hold for them.

Bas was occupied with doctoral studies at Utrecht University, with a view to obtaining a higher degree. Jo worked for a newspaper publishing company in Amsterdam. Sometimes Bas would pay her a surprise visit in her private office. She also wrote short stories in her spare time.

In the 1930s the use of the motor car by the masses was still in the future and many people used the bicycle for long

Bas and Jo made their first home in a flat overlooking a canal like this one

journeys. One year Bas spent several weeks exploring the historical riches of England on his bike. Jo met him in Wales after visiting southern England. In 1936 he spent six months using his bicycle to reach Palestine. He thought that as a Christian minister he should see the places associated with Jesus' life on earth.

Early Days in the Ministry

In September 1937 Bas was appointed assistant pastor at the Reformed Church in Badhoevedorp, just a short distance north of Amsterdam's Schiphol Airport. This appointment ended in October 1938, by which time the synod, or governing authority in the wider church, judged him to be well prepared to take on a church of his own at Nieuw Beerta. This was a parish in the province of Groningen, in the far north of the Netherlands, about an hour's bicycle ride from the German border. Bas was pastor there from 1938 to 1944.

A Groningen windmill

Nieuw Beerta was a tough rural parish. The landscape was flat and dotted with windmills. Many of the people were farmers. Bas found that most of the congregation of his new church had either fallen away or become Communists. The Aders threw themselves into the work with zeal. They prayed and worked together.

Bas believed the great truths of the historic faith. He believed that at the centre of Christianity stands a cross, a sign of sacrifice and suffering. In his own words, 'The Sinless One took our guilt upon himself and atoned for our sins with his blood, and he did so because we had no power to save ourselves.'

Rev. Berkelbach van der Sprenkel said that Bastiaan Ader had a 'passion for souls'. He organized all sorts of meetings, including those for Bible

*A modern photograph of
Nieuw Beerta Church*

study and for young people. He engaged in outreach to local villages, and he and Jo were known for their hospitality and their real love and care for the people. Though there was no dramatic increase in numbers, gradually folk began coming to hear this new preacher. Jo decided to study for the examinations that would enable her to qualify as an official 'church worker', in order to expand her knowledge of the church's teaching and practice. This meant that she could to some extent take Bas's place if he should be away for any reason. In these and other ways, the Aders cheerfully undertook the reviving and rebuilding of the congregation.

There was one event from this period that is worthy of note. Poland had been overrun by the Germans in September 1939, and some Polish prisoners were being held in a camp in Germany, not far from the border with the Netherlands. On a snowy day in the winter of 1939–40, a Polish captain, a sergeant and two other men escaped from the German camp, wrapped in white blankets for camouflage, and crossed over into the neutral Netherlands. The Aders helped them and Bas pleaded on their behalf in a court in The Hague, supporting their request to be allowed to go to France, where they wanted to continue the struggle against Germany. Eventually, Bas received a note from the captain telling of their safe arrival in Paris. He wished to thank Bas for his help in securing their release. This was not the last time that they were to hear from this captain.

Occupation by the Nazis

In 1940 the German army decided to make a speedy assault on the Anglo-French forces in France and Belgium. The proposed route involved the violation of neutral Dutch territory. On 10 May 1940, without issuing a declaration of war, élite units of the German army parachuted into the most important centres of power in the Netherlands. With key points secured, the way was then clear for a massive army to cross into the country, which up till then had remained neutral (as it had been during the First World War). In less than a week, the Dutch were forced to surrender. The Dutch Queen Wilhelmina (who had granted asylum to the exiled German Kaiser after the end of the First World War, allowing him, with his family and entourage, to live in luxury at Doorn, near Amsterdam) was forced to escape to England in a British warship. Five years

An early emblem of the NSB (Dutch Nazis)

of illegal and cruel occupation were to follow. Neutrality, and even kindness towards an exiled emperor, paid no dividends when dealing with Nazi Germany!

In 1940 the population of the Netherlands was over 8.5 million. Various sections of the community reacted differently to the German invasion. The majority were outraged by it. Gradually resistance groups developed. However, a tiny Dutch Nazi Party (the NSB) had been in existence ever since the early 1930s, and after 1940 over 100,000 people joined this party. Although they were only a minority, their loyalty to the Nazi cause was dangerous to the resistance movement. Being Dutch, it was easy for them to mingle with, and even to infiltrate, any group which resisted German policies in the Netherlands.

From the very beginning of the occupation the Germans made no attempt to treat the subdued Dutch with any consideration. For instance, clocks had to

The German army used this type of aircraft (Ju 52) to drop parachutists

be adjusted by an hour and forty minutes to bring the time in the Netherlands into line with that in Germany. The message was simple: 'Your nation is now absorbed into the German Reich. We do not recognize your separate existence.' That was a mere pinprick compared with what was to come.

The Persecution of the Jews

In the years since Hitler's rise to power in Germany in 1933, approximately 34,000 Jews had emigrated from that country to the Netherlands to escape the cruel persecution by the Nazis. More than 15,000 of these immigrants were still living there in 1940, at the time of the German occupation, along with 140,000 native Dutch Jews.

Bas and Jo were particularly distressed by the anti-Jewish laws which the occupying Nazi forces now began to implement in the Netherlands. The mass murder of Jewish people revolted them. The Synod of the Dutch Reformed Church circulated a message among their pastors that was to be read out to all congregations. It boldly opposed persecution of the Jews. Bas was pleased to read this statement out to his people. Soon afterwards, one of Bas and Jo's relatives was on a train going to Groningen when he overheard some NSB members talking among themselves. One of them mentioned the minister of Nieuw Beerta Church and said that he was 'a bad influence on young people'. Someone said, 'He must be got out of the way.' Bas was already a marked man.

On 19 April 1942 the Aders' first son, Bas Jan, was born. The welfare of the young baby would be an important factor in any decisions Bas made from now on. Should he wait for the Allies to rescue them from German tyranny? Should he do nothing more dangerous than listen secretly to the news on the BBC (British Broadcasting Corporation)? Bas reasoned that if he were a citizen of an Allied nation fighting the Germans, like Britain or America, he could be called on to join the armed services. Thousands of men were being conscripted to fight. The Allies were losing men in the fighting every day. Most of these men had families who were devoted to them, just as he had. He came to the conclusion that, in spite of the risks, it was his moral duty to resist Nazi rule in any way open to him. To put it simply, Bas was not content to remain passive and await rescue at the cost of the blood of the Allied forces.

It was German policy to try to gather all the Dutch Jews into Amsterdam. From there they were almost always sent to Westerbork in the north-east of the Netherlands. This was a camp from which trainloads of prisoners, mostly Jewish, were sent east for annihilation.

Bas received a letter from a Jewish photographer, who had worked in the publishing office with Jo, and who is referred to in Jo's post-war book as Lily, though this was not her real name. Jo and Lily had become friends. Lily had taken photographs at Bas and Jo's wedding. She had also shared a meal at their home overlooking the canal. The letter said, 'Can I come and stay with you for a while? I am in great need.' Lily was not exaggerating. She was scheduled for interrogation by the Gestapo. After that she would be taken to a train waiting for her at Westerbork. For Lily, Bas and Jo's response would mean life or death.

Faced with her request, Bas and Jo asked themselves, 'What would Jesus do?' Bas was reminded that a Jew had sacrificed himself on the cross for the salvation of Jo and himself, both of whom were Gentiles. The story of the Good Samaritan came to mind. The only possible

A typical scene of a deportation

answer was, 'Come'. Their manse, the house provided by the church for their use as a family, was now about to serve a different purpose.

Lily brought no ration cards with her, but obtaining food was a comparatively minor problem. Most of the men who comprised the church council of elders and deacons were local farmers. Bas had built a bomb shelter to provide safety for the family when Allied aircraft bombed the nearby German port of Emden. There was danger because German shrapnel and stray British bombs had fallen around the house. The bomb shelter, as they called it, could also serve to house animals, such as the two pigs which were currently occupying it.

Conversation with Lily revealed that she had a friend 'Esther', a typist, who was in similar danger. Bas and Jo looked at each other. Both had the same thought. Bas was the first to put it into words: 'Then she must come as well. The risk with two is the same as with one.' He was right.

This was the church house (manse) where the Aders hid both Christians and Jews

Hiding the Jewish girls in the loft involved detailed planning. Who *needed* to know about them? Local 'safe places' were organized in case the house was searched by enemy forces. They decided that they would always refer to the refugees as 'mice', and never as people. For instance, they would say, 'We have mice in the attic.' There would be DPDs—Daily Panic Drills—and so on …

Soon two people in the attics had to become three. Short of workers, the Germans started rounding up young Dutch men to carry out slave labour for the Third Reich. Many loyal young Dutch folk were determined to resist this policy if possible. Jo had a sister who had died in childbirth. Her son Chris was now studying to be a vet at Utrecht University. To avoid deportation in the summer of 1943, he fled to Nieuw Beerta for sanctuary.

Only about a month later Frits, the son of Jo's deceased older brother Johan, came asking for help. He was an architecture student in the same unenviable position as Chris. That made four people hiding in the church house. The young men had to share a room upstairs, and all had to maintain absolute silence during daylight hours.

As the life-and-death nature of the German occupation became clearer to Bas, he became more involved in active, rather than passive, resistance. Frequently he was away from home working with resistance groups. He had false papers giving him the identity of Gerard van Zaanen. He dressed as a farm worker, or in other appropriate clothing, according to the description given in the false identity papers he was using at the time. He journeyed regularly to Amsterdam; he organized hiding places other than his own home for those who had no money or contacts; he brought food coupons to those he had hidden; he also brought them news and encouraged them.

Bas even persuaded the reluctant Jo to receive two more Jewish girls into the house, whom they referred to as 'Mirjam' and 'Naomi'. As with Lily and Esther, these were not their real names; all the refugees were given pseudonyms for security reasons.

On the few occasions when he came home, Jo was distressed to notice that Bas was looking exhausted. This was hardly surprising, since it is generally agreed that he was responsible for saving over 200 lives in all. The exact figures and details will never be known, as no records were kept, in case of seizure by the enemy.

After the war Naomi, whose real name was Johanna-Ruth Dobschiner (Hansie to friends), wrote a book in which she recorded her memories of Bas. Thus we have a vivid first-hand account of the way he worked. Hansie was an eighteen-year-old nurse in the Jewish Hospital in Amsterdam. Shortly before every doctor, nurse and patient was taken away to the death camps, she learned from the hall porter in the hospital that she had been selected to go into hiding, or 'selected to live', as she later described the experience.

It was 8 September 1943. Wearing her nurse's uniform, she was to leave the hospital after lunch as if going for a casual walk. The porter gave her an address to which she was to go. She had to memorize it and not write anything down. As she approached the street corner, she was to use her right hand to take out a handkerchief. At the precise moment she turned the corner, she was to sneeze into the handkerchief. From then on she must use her handbag to cover up the star she was wearing on her clothing, which identified her as Jewish.

When she went into the house, she met the tallest man she had ever seen. With a kind, seemingly relaxed manner, he told her that he was going to change her name to Francisca Dobber, Frans for short. An unknown lady appeared and cut the star off Hansie's clothing. Bas (for it was he) then went out of the room. The lady invited Hansie to change into a red flannel dress, which fortunately fitted her. 'I'll take care of your uniform', she was told. Bas instructed her to accompany him to the tram stop and then on the train and, since she spoke fluent German, to speak only in that language, even if other Dutch passengers looked disgusted when they heard them talking in German.

When they reached the station nearest his house, Bas put his fingers in his mouth and produced an excellent imitation of the piercing call of a nocturnal bird. A big policeman appeared out of the darkness bringing two bicycles. Hansie overheard the policeman telling Bas that somebody whom they both knew needed 200 ration books, identity cards and inkpads. After cycling in the dark for nearly an hour across flat countryside, Bas and Hansie finally arrived at a house. Once inside, she met the other refugees and, of course, the woman she would come to know as 'Aunt Jo'.

Yad Vashem is Israel's official organization set up to recognize the victims of the Holocaust, and those who helped them. One of its researchers, Mordecai Paldiel, unearthed the details surrounding the rescue of two other Jewish people. Bas went to the Joodsche Invalide Hospital and was told that Josephine Ganor and her friend, referred to as 'Mep who worked in the kitchen', were in imminent danger. He asked his parents to give them sanctuary in their home in Groningen. In this way two people found life and safety from September 1943 to May 1944. From this it is clear that his parents were in strong sympathy with his activities.

Bas was also keen to help the Allied cause in other ways. He provided dignified burials in the churchyard for at least five British and US airmen who had been shot down. Others, who parachuted to safety, were given as much help as possible to evade capture. No details of these activities have survived, because little or nothing could be written down at the time. Helping such aircrew obviously added to the risks Bas faced.

The threat closes in

It was Easter in April 1944. Bas gave his coded knock on the back door of the manse. Everybody assembled in the kitchen. Bas looked pale from loss of sleep and lack of food. There was serious news. Orders for his arrest had been circulated. All the refugees must scatter immediately according to prearranged plans. Their new hideouts, if they could reach

Three Jewish people being transported to a Concentration Camp

them, would eventually be in the province of Limburg in the far south of the Netherlands. The Allied armies were not far away from that area.

Lily, Esther and Bas's helper Wil, all of whom were Jewish, were caught. Some time later a letter arrived from the Polish captain who had escaped from the German camp and crossed into the Netherlands at the beginning of the war. In it he said:

> As I was standing on the station at W. on Friday afternoon, a long train full of Jews from Westerbork came near. From one of the cattle wagons, behind an opening with barbed wire stretched across it, three ladies called out to me. I could not get very near to them because the whole platform was filled with ORPO [Ordnungspolizei—police responsible for law enforcement throughout the Third Reich]. They were holding people back from the train. Even so I was able to get a bit closer. These poor people wanted desperately to tell me

something. I made out your name and address. They wanted to greet you once more. I am happy to pass this message to you.

Sincerely

Captain K.

It was Jo who received this letter because Bas was by now a hunted man. Her immediate distress was caused by the thought that they had sheltered Lily and Esther for nearly two years, only for them to be seen peering out of a cattle truck which was on its way to a concentration camp, probably in Poland. All the refugees had asked for Bibles and all had a long personal letter from Bas, full of spiritual comfort. Clutching the captain's letter, Jo ran to a quiet place and prayed through her tears that the girls would have faith in Jesus as they faced the final trial of death. It was Jesus who said, 'I am the resurrection, and the life: he that believeth in me, though he were dead, yet shall he live: and whosoever liveth and believeth in me shall never die' (John 11:25 26).

However, Jo was happy to know that others whom they had sheltered and helped did not share the same fate. Hansie, for instance, reached Limburg and eventual freedom. While in hiding she became a Christian. To the end of her life she looked back to the time when she was hiding in Bas and Jo's home as a crucial stage in her spiritual pilgrimage. After all, it was there she had first read the New Testament and received the Bible through which she learned of her need for a personal relationship with Jesus Christ.

Arrest

It was 30 May 1944. The manse was surrounded by ORPO with loaded rifles and their NSB helpers. Bas had already been gone for nearly seven weeks. Jo was expecting another baby. Nevertheless, she was interrogated and held in custody for a time. She was eventually released on condition that she stayed in the house.

One day Miss Van der Pol, the church worker assigned by the synod to help with the spiritual needs of the parish, came with grim news. She did not seem to be her usual self and Jo guessed what had happened. 'Has

Bas been arrested?' she asked tonelessly. One nod said it all. A policeman, Klaas Rodermond, who was secretly a member of the NSB, had won Bas's confidence over a considerable period of time before eventually betraying him. Jo was told later that he may have been induced to do this by a promise of promotion.

Bas was held in prison in Haarlem. During the interrogation he was beaten with a truncheon. His nose was broken and his ear drum damaged. But he revealed no secrets, no hiding places and no names, whether of Jews or of resistance helpers, either then or later. Bas was so important that the Dutch resistance drew up a plan to free him from prison. Sadly, the day before the proposed raid on the jail, he was moved to the Gestapo prison in Amsterdam. From here there was no hope of escape.

The church council members advised Jo to leave the house. She cycled from one minister's house to another, finally reaching Winschoten, where she gave birth to her second son, Erik, in November 1944.

The house belonging to the Nieuw Beerta church was pillaged by members of the NSB and ORPO. They stole everything worth having, including a 200-year-old spinet (a small type of harpsichord), which had been a family heirloom.

Smuggled Correspondence

With the cooperation of Dutch sympathizers, Bas was able to smuggle out letters to Jo. They were written on toilet paper. He wrote, 'I am happy to have my pocket Bible here. It has given me so much comfort.' He recalled that 25 September 1944 was their ninth wedding anniversary. Nor did he forget that Psalm 27 was their 'wedding psalm'. Remarkably, he could say, 'I have experienced what the psalm talks about.' The opening verse of the psalm says, 'The Lord is my light and my salvation; whom shall I fear? The Lord is the strength of my life; of whom shall I be afraid?' Further on it says, '... in the time of trouble God shall hide me ... he shall set me up on a rock.' For somebody in Bas's predicament, and with his strong faith, such words, and others in the psalm, would be an encouragement.

Like the apostle Paul, he made an attempt to set up a church in the prison. This was done by smuggling simple sermons and other messages to other Dutch prisoners.

He wrote a long poem addressed to Jo, complete with a melody, in which he expresses his confidence in the Lord. He wrote, 'I have never been so close to God.' He exhorted Jo: 'Let us think about each other and pray for each other a lot.' He insisted that though it had led to his being in prison, he could not have acted in a different way. Mass murder and unprovoked tyranny must be resisted. One letter ends: 'Give kisses to the children from me. I hope all is well with both of them.' The previous sentence reveals that he knew that a second child had been born.

Another letter expresses his concern for his parents and their well-being. He puts on record how grateful he is to them for sharing the gospel with him in his early life. His faith in Christ as his Saviour gave him the certainty of eternal life. Such assurance was priceless to him while languishing in a Nazi prison. His parents knew he was imprisoned. The strain on them must have been hard to imagine, let alone experience. The stress probably took its toll. His mother lived on for some years after the war was over, but his father died before the end of the war from a heart condition.

A Reprisal

In November 1944 a German was injured by a shot from a hostile Dutchman. The Germans decided to shoot Dutch prisoners as a reprisal. On the rainy night of 20 November 1944, sixteen days after the birth of his second son and just over a month before his thirty-fifth birthday, Bas was shot in secrecy at Veenendaal, along with five others. He asked the officer in charge that he should be executed last so that he could minister the Word of God to the other prisoners. This request was motivated by the desire to make sure that the other five were given comfort and prepared for their journey to the next world. The Dutch people who buried Bas opened his bag and found in it his small Bible and a hymn book. Other Dutch people transported his body from Veenendaal to the family grave at Driebergen.

Jo, who lived until 1994, wrote, 'By risking his own life he had helped and served others who were in need. It stands written in John chapter 15: "Greater love hath no man than this, that a man lay down his life for his friends." What was valid for the first Christians, and for the last Christians as well, was valid for Bas.'

Bas's grave in the Loenen Field of Honour

More Information on Bastiaan Ader

Jo Ader-Appels' book *Een Groninger Pastorie in de Storm* was published by T. Wever, Franeker in 1947 (ISBN 90–6135–214–2). I hope Dutch people who were interested by this story will acquire this book. Betty Holt, herself the author of several books, translated it into English. Without Mrs Holt's kindness and hard work, it would be impossible to write about Bastiaan Ader in the English language. Sadly, it has not yet been published in English.

Most of the refugees and other characters mentioned in Jo Ader-Appels' book are referred to only by pseudonyms. However the Israeli Commemorative Centre, Yad Vashem, states that the real name of 'Lily' was Nettie Samuels.

Johanna-Ruth Dobschiner wrote a post-war book of memories called *Selected to Live*, published by Pickering and Inglis in 1968 (ISBN 0–7208–2044–8). The story of her life is told with extra detail in *War and Grace*, published by Evangelical Press in 2005 (ISBN-13 978–0–85234–594–8/ISBN 0–85234–594–1). When referring to Bas, *War and Grace* uses the spelling Bastian, not Bastiaan. Bastian was used and favoured by Hansie Dobschiner, but her attempt to anglicize the name is technically incorrect.

On 22 November 1967 Yad Vashem recognized Bas and Jo Ader as

'Righteous Among the Nations'. There is an account of the Aders' work, and how they are commemorated, on the Internet site:

http://db.yadvashem.org/righteous/family.html?language=en&item Id=4042995

Erik Ader, the second son of Bas and Jo, has supplied information not available in any source known to me, and I am therefore, indebted to him for his help. Mr Ader also owns the copyright of the photographs of his parents and the Manse.

There is a book largely about the artistic work of the first son of Bas and Jo called *Bas Jan Ader: Death is Elsewhere* by Alexander Dumbadze. It was published by the University of Chicago Press in 2013. ISBN-13: 978–0–226–03853–7. Those readers interested in the life of this man will find a number of web sites devoted to assessments of his unusual artistic productions.

Rachmiel Frydland: Holocaust survivor

'The worst place a man could be in World War II was Central Europe, and the worst country was Poland; the worst religion a man could have was Judaism, and perhaps the worst form of Judaism was Hebrew Christianity … Rachmiel Frydland wandered for years through burning Poland, dazed, bewildered, but always spared.'

These words are part of Zola Levitt's introduction to Rachmiel Frydland's autobiography, which tells the true story of his experiences in Poland before and during the Second World War. There were very few Holocaust survivors from war-ravaged Poland, so it is especially important that this account should be preserved for posterity. The world needs to know the truth about events that many would prefer to forget.

A strict Jewish upbringing

Rachmiel Frydland was born 'before Passover' in 1919 into a very devout orthodox Jewish family. They lived in a tiny village in a forest about four miles east of Chelm in the Lublin district of Poland. His four sisters were Rachel, Rebecca, Esther and Judith. His father, Abraham, always wore traditional Jewish religious clothing, and had a beard, side curls and all the customary marks of Jewish orthodoxy. They were a poverty-stricken family who eked out a living by buying produce from local peasant farmers, and selling it to nearby townspeople. They were little more than street traders.

Their dwelling was divided into three parts, one of which served as a barn.

As the only son, Rachmiel was well instructed in the orthodox Jewish faith. He was taught to recite prayers in childhood, long before he knew what the words meant. Even when he was old enough to understand Hebrew, his prayers were still just formulas said by rote, without any attention to the meaning.

Traditional Jewish religious clothing similar to that which Rachmiel both saw and used

All the Jewish Holy Days were observed in detail. For instance, on New Year's Eve Abraham would buy a slice of pineapple, dip it in honey, give a small portion to everyone in the family, and recite in Hebrew, 'May it be God's will that this be a good and sweet year.'

Eating on the eve of the solemn Day of Atonement was as much an obligation and a sign of orthodoxy as fasting was on the following day. Young Rachmiel looked forward to the eve of this most important day because he knew there would be a rare chicken dinner at the end of the rituals. Abraham made sure that the females in the family were given a hen and the males a cockerel. The fowls were waved over their heads and the following words recited three times in Hebrew: 'This is my atonement; this is my ransom; this is offered in exchange for me. The chicken will be put to death, and I will go instead to meet a good, long and peaceful life.'

The religious life was followed in the greatest detail possible. Sadly, the Jewish community was prejudiced against their Gentile neighbours, looking on them as worshippers of images and idols. There would be fights between Jewish and Gentile boys. When this happened the Jews called the Gentiles 'unclean', while the Jews in turn were regarded by their neighbours as unacceptably different, separate and unusual.

When Rachmiel was growing up, the Polish state required all children to attend school from the age of eight. However, Rachmiel's father did not want his only son to be influenced by non-Jewish ideas. As a result he kept finding excuses to avoid the Polish government's school attendance rules. Instead of secular studies, Rachmiel was educated by rabbis, and when he was nine, he was enrolled in a Jewish religious training school in nearby Chelm.

He attended this Jewish school until he was thirteen. At that age, an important milestone for Jewish boys, he became Bar Mitzvah, a 'Son of the Law'. The ceremony marking this event made him a member of the synagogue. Prior to that, according to Jewish tradition, his father was held responsible for the sins of his son, but now that he had become a 'Son of the Law', he was regarded as 'a man', and would therefore have to pay the penalty for his own misdeeds.

After the Bar Mitzvah, Abraham Frydland discussed his son's future with teachers and relatives, and decided that he should become a rabbi. This involved enrolling Rachmiel in a rabbinical school in Warsaw, Poland's capital. There were several such schools in Warsaw, all sponsored financially by rich Jewish people.

Students at the rabbinical schools had to memorize the Talmud. This book, which is regarded as the most sacred of all by the Jewish people, is not the same as the Hebrew Old Testament (which forms part of the Bible), but comprises the whole body of Jewish civil and ceremonial law, as interpreted by the rabbis, and stories from Jewish history. There was no opportunity for discussion of what they learned, and any students who entertained doubts or had queries would not confide in their teachers.

From Rachmiel's point of view the next two years were a misery. He was bored by the ritualistic learning of the Talmud. Strict discipline was something he could accept, but the old rabbi in charge disliked Rachmiel, and constantly referred to him in front of the other teenagers as 'the Chelmer fool'. This man was also prone to fits of bad temper which left Rachmiel humiliated and depressed.

Eventually Rachmiel moved to a less rigid rabbinical school in Warsaw's

Gnoina Street. At this school meals were taken in a local restaurant. This arrangement brought Rachmiel into contact with ordinary city people. Inadvertently, the other customers made him feel uncomfortable. This was probably because he was dressed in a long black robe with fringes, wore the traditional Jewish head covering and had side curls.

The growing rebellion in Rachmiel's heart concerned small things at first. Were the Gentiles really as terrible as his teachers said? Must the discipline in the rabbinical schools be so unfeeling? Why did Christians believe in the Jewish prophets? He also read things in the Talmud which discouraged him. One concerned a very devout rabbi, called ben Zakkai, who wept when he knew his death was imminent because he was uncertain where he would spend eternity. Rachmiel thought, 'If this pious Jew is uncertain about his entry into heaven, then what hope is there for me?'

In 1936, disillusioned with an educational method in which no questions were permitted and with a curriculum based solely on the Talmud, he left rabbinical school and never returned. The desire to learn things outside this very restricted area of study had become irresistible.

Attitude to Christianity

Rachmiel's thinking was saturated with orthodox Jewish views of Jesus. It was considered a sin even to speak his name and he was referred to as 'the Hanged One'. The Talmud includes a book called 'The History of Jesus', composed in the Middle Ages, which claimed that Jesus was an illegitimate child, that he forced his mother Mary to admit this, and that he had learned sorcery in Egypt. These tales, and other derogatory stories along the same lines, were all accepted as true by many of the rabbis and other readers of the Talmud.

Rachmiel was seventeen when he left the rabbinical school. He was now in Warsaw on his own, selling items of clothing in the street, and lodging with a friendly family called the Grikers. They owned a tailoring business. The Grikers told their lodger that they liked to go and argue with 'missionaries'. Surely Rachmiel, who had studied so much, would be able to tell them the truth about these people?

The Great Change

One evening in 1937 Rachmiel accompanied the Grikers to a meeting, at which about forty people were present. The speaker was Paul Rosenberg, a Jew who had become a Christian. He stated that there were hundreds of prophecies in the Old Testament about Jesus, who was the long-awaited Messiah of Israel. After the meeting was over, Rachmiel produced contradictory interpretations of all but one of the Bible passages he had quoted. The exception was Daniel 9:26. At the end of that verse it says, '... the Messiah shall be cut off [killed], but not for himself'. Rachmiel was not satisfied with the Jewish contention that this was a reference to King Agrippa. Since Messiah had to be a descendant of David, that view was untenable. Spiritual doubts were beginning to set in.

Around this time Rachmiel was given a New Testament in Hebrew. He found, as Paul Rosenberg had said, that hundreds of messianic prophecies from the Old Testament were fulfilled by events in the life of Jesus Christ.

Rachmiel returned to the mission. This time a Gentile woman, Tordis Christofferson, was speaking compellingly about the temple in Jerusalem, explaining how its design, furniture and fittings all had spiritual meanings. As a religious Jew, Rachmiel would recite two prayers every morning: first, 'Blessed be the Lord God ... who did not make me a Gentile', and, second, 'Blessed be the Lord God ... who did not make me a woman'. Yet here was a Gentile woman calling for repentance from sin and for prayer!

Rachmiel had always been accustomed to stand for prayer, but feeling an urgent need to pray, he overcame his reluctance and, as he later recorded, 'I knelt with others and poured out my heart before God asking him to be merciful to me, a proud and selfish sinner. This was my conversion from unforgiven sins to the acceptance of the sacrifice of the Lord Jesus on the cross ... As I read the Hebrew New Testament, I realized that the apostle Paul must have had a personal relationship with his Messiah, such as I had never experienced. My outward conditions did not matter now. All that mattered was the state of my heart and the Messiah. As I prayed my spirit was made alive and changed within me … a veil had been over my eyes, but now that was stripped away. I was a new creation in Messiah Jesus: "… old things are passed away; behold, all things are become new" (2 Corinthians 5:17).'

Afterwards, when he met friends, they would often comment, 'You have changed.' Rachmiel wrote, 'I kept silent, for it was difficult to explain what had really happened … but I knew for certain that the Lord Jesus was my personal Saviour, Lord, and King.' Things took on a new significance from that important moment in 53 Ogrodowa Street, Warsaw.

Rachmiel Frydland had been a Christian for two years when the Second World War started. For him, these were useful, happy years. He had English lessons. He did church work. His parents had been told by other Jews that if he converted to Christianity, he would take a new name and would have a cross branded on his left arm. They were comforted to discover that none of these rumours was true. However, things were about to change in other ways.

Nazi Brutality

The Nazi invasion of Poland on 1 September 1939 marked the official start of the Second World War. Within a month Poland was crushed and humiliated. The Germans held a triumphant victory parade in Warsaw.

Rachmiel decided to leave the city. Reaching the outskirts, he was stopped by a fanatical member of an élite Nazi fighting unit called the SS, who shouted at him, 'Are you a Jew?' Without answering, Rachmiel showed the soldier a document confirming that he was a member of the German Baptist Church. The SS officer merely glanced at the certificate and said, 'Yes, but you are still a Jew.' He then picked up a shovel and hit Rachmiel on his back so hard that he fell into a ditch. The shovel was then thrown into the ditch beside him. He was ordered to stay in the ditch with other Jews. They were being made to bury dead horses, which had been killed in the recent fighting when Polish cavalry had charged to attack oncoming German tanks. This was Rachmiel's first taste of Nazi brutality towards the Jews.

German victory parade in Warsaw, 1939

More was to come. In the summer of 1940 he was walking to Chelm from his parents' house, where he was staying at the time. Some German soldiers, who were drunk, stopped him and beat him senseless for no reason at all. When he was able, he dragged himself, bleeding badly, into Chelm. Friends insisted that he should see a doctor immediately. The doctor gave him little hope because the wounds were deep and full of dirt and dust and there was a serious risk of blood poisoning. The cuts were cleaned and bandages applied, but complications set in. Rachmiel could eat nothing and vomited blood for many days. To the surprise of his friends, he eventually recovered.

It was not long before the laws relating to the approximately three million Jews in Poland started to take effect. Jews were compelled to display the Star of David on their clothing. They were forbidden to use public transport. Ghettos sprang up in the towns and cities where the Jews were housed. Anybody trying to escape from a ghetto was liable to be shot. Jews who lived in the countryside had to remain in their villages. Identity documents had to be carried at all times. If a German soldier approached as they were walking in the street, Jews had to take off their hats and step off the pavement into the roadway. Rachmiel was short-sighted, and on one occasion he failed to notice a Nazi soldier. The blow he received as a result of failing to give way and remove his hat knocked him senseless and broke his spectacles. For the rest of the war he had to manage without glasses. Nor did he ever wear a hat again.

Even attendance at the church of which he was a member was forbidden to him. The pastor who had formerly preached the Word of God now used his message to celebrate Hitler's victory in conquering France. Rachmiel was told that this church was not for Jewish Christians and that people like him had been transferred to other churches. He was unwelcome at the German Baptist Church and was not to return.

A Jew has his beard forcibly cut off

In June 1941 Germany used Poland as a base from which to launch a surprise attack on the Soviet Union. The preparations for this assault included building a road from Chelm to Dorohusk, which was near the border with the USSR. When completed, it would be used by German forces as they struck east against the Russians.

The Germans decreed that Jews and some Poles should be compelled to build the road. Rachmiel was one of the forced labourers sent to do this work. For a week or two the camp where they were made to live was largely unguarded. Then the camp was surrounded by a fence and carefully guarded. No food was given to the workers and some died as a result. Starvation was imminent, so Rachmiel escaped, but was caught and cruelly beaten. He was so hungry that he decided to escape again.

He chose a Sunday, so that if he survived the bullets and the subsequent manhunt, he could go to a nearby church, where he knew he would be welcome. At this church the Bible was preached and obeyed. He climbed the fence, and reached safety. He arrived at the church just in time for the communion service!

Once the war between Germany and the Soviet Union began, the search for him was called off. In this way, he survived imminent death yet again. None of these brutalities was as bad as what was to come.

The 'Final Solution'

In January 1942, senior Nazis met in conference at Wannsee, near Berlin, to deal with what they called 'the Jewish Problem'. Important decisions that would lead to the mass-murder of Jews, and others, were made at this meeting. Rachmiel Frydland, of course, knew nothing of this at the time. If the persecution of Jews, and the fact that many of them were being put to death, had been obvious before Wannsee, from 1942 onwards the question of survival

Barricades confine Jews inside the ghetto

became infinitely harder for him and his fellow Jews. Poland was now systematically combed for Jews. The search was carried out so thoroughly that hardly any survived.

On 30 August 1942 Rachmiel Frydland was ordered to join a train which he knew was heading to Sobibor concentration camp. He fled into the forest. If he was caught, he could expect to be killed on the spot for any one of six reasons:

1. He was a Jew.

2. He had escaped.

3. He was away from his official place of residence.

4. He was not wearing on his clothing the star which identified him as a Jew.

5. He had used public transport.

6. He had no personal documents.

Resigned to the fact that he was likely to die at any moment, he nevertheless managed to escape from the Nazis on numerous occasions when death seemed certain. Being young and strong, he found work on various small farms, surviving on meagre rations and never staying long in one place. Times were so grim, and the stress so overwhelming, that frequently he would have genuinely welcomed death.

Eventually he was arrested and put in a slave labour camp in the village of Saycice. The camp was guarded by black-uniformed SS guards armed with machine guns. He managed to jump over the wall of the well from which the camp drew water and escaped. In spite of the hail of bullets and the subsequent search, he found himself alive and free.

Sometimes he received unexpected help. In Chelm he knew the house where a Christian family, the Olichwiers, lived. He knocked on their front door. When they opened it, he told them he was weary of being hunted. He just wanted to surrender to what now seemed inevitable. His wish was to have a time of prayer with them, and then to be given directions to the local Gestapo (secret police) headquarters. They refused to help him give himself up. Rachmiel was dirty, and dressed in rags. At great risk to themselves, the Olichwiers burned his filthy clothing, gave him soap and water and provided him with new clothes which had Ukrainian embroidery on them. He could now pass as a non-Jew. In order to protect the Olichwiers from persecution, he left their house as soon as he could.

During the vicious war between Germany and the Soviet Union, millions of Russian prisoners were routinely starved, or put to death in other ways. However, White Russians, who were not Communists, would not automatically be killed by the Nazis. Rachmiel's friend Pastor Ivanov was a White Russian. The pastor's wife was able to acquire the documents of a certain Ivan Petruschuk, a White Russian who had died. She handed his papers to Rachmiel and said, 'Now you are no longer Rachmiel Frydland. You are Ivan Petruschuk.' With these documents, he would be easier to help than if he were a known Jew. If he was given shelter or work, anyone who was later apprehended and charged with aiding him could claim that he had shown his identity papers. The ruse was effective.

Once the Germans had crushed the Jewish revolt in the Warsaw Ghetto in May 1943, they began to believe that there were few, if any, Polish Jews still left alive. As a result, the searches in Poland became less rigorous. As the war with Soviet Russia became more costly to the Germans, they even stopped paying bounties to those who handed over Jews to the authorities for execution. Previously Polish people who did this had been allowed to retain the property and possessions of the Jews who had been taken away for annihilation.

Finally, freedom came. It was early in 1945 when the armies of the USSR, supported by the Allies, swept the Nazis out of Poland. Rachmiel Frydland was no longer hunted, and no longer condemned to die solely on the grounds that he was Jewish. Although he was only twenty-five, he felt old. Searches for his family proved futile. His parents, sisters and all his other known relatives were dead. The Nazi persecution in Poland had been exceptionally horrendous and thorough. He had emerged from the ordeal by a series of minor miracles. At least, that was how it seemed to him. He wrote, 'Death, my constant companion, had little fear for me anymore.' Sometimes he speculated whether he had survived in order to tell the world the truth about the Holocaust.

The Post-War Years

The immediate post-war years brought new dangers. Stalin was determined that Poland should have a Communist government, not an elected one. A local war broke out between Polish Nationalists and Polish Communists. At one point Rachmiel was detained by Nationalist troops who demanded proof that he was not a Jewish Communist. Although it was no longer illegal, it was still not a good thing to be Jewish. Backed by the victorious armies of the USSR, it was inevitable that the Communists would eventually seize power.

When the post-war turbulence had settled down sufficiently, Rachmiel and a colleague did itinerant work for the churches as required. After a while the President of the Polish Evangelical Church offered him the pastorate of a church in the west of the country. He responded, 'How could I pastor others when I had just emerged from a nightmare of death, and had not yet found my bearings?' A suitable period of study was required before he could undertake any such responsibility. After all, he had never received even the most basic education in either secular or biblical matters.

With the help of two British Hebrew Christians, he was accepted to study in England at All Nations Bible College, starting in October 1947. Concerning this he wrote, 'I studied avidly … I took to books like a thirsty person goes to a water fountain … Bible College studies were not enough for me … I found that I could study for London University examinations as an extra challenge.' He earned a degree in Semitic Languages and a higher degree in Medieval and Talmudic Hebrew.

Ministry and Writings

From 1952 to 1961 he worked in the United States, having crossed the Atlantic in the *Queen Elizabeth*. Rachmiel had been asked by Hermon House, a Hebrew Christian Centre in Manhattan, New York, to take the lead in its work. He did this gladly until 1961 when an opportunity came to fulfil an ambition by going to Israel. Sponsored by the International Hebrew Christian Alliance, he was keen to bring unity to the few hundred Jewish Christians who lived there.

On arrival in Haifa, he found that the word 'Jew' opened all doors. Automatically, Jewish immigrants were given a home, a job, Israeli citizenship and help in every other way. However, those who professed to be Jewish *Christians* soon found a different side to the Israeli state. A Hebrew Christian in Israel is subject to pressure and rejection. He or she is thought of as a person who has ceased to be Jewish. For such a person to return to Israel is regarded as being there under false pretences. A Jew may be an atheist, a Communist, or even a criminal, but not a Christian! To be a Christian is deemed to be the equivalent of a Gentile, a non-Jew, an apostate.

Rachmiel was so dismayed by Israeli policies that on his return to the US in August 1964, he set about writing a book called *A Hebrew Christian Looks at Israel*. When this was published in America a year later, it brought him criticism and hostility—not only from Israel, but also from many Jewish people living in North America. Rachmiel himself was simply opposed to pressure and persecution wherever these things were to be found. His hope and prayer was that the state of Israel would change its treatment of its Jewish Christian minority.

He had gone to Israel alone, but he returned to America with a wife, Estelle, and two children (they would have four children in all). On his return to America, he became Professor of Jewish Studies at Tennessee Temple Schools for seven years. From 1973 to the end of his life, he was minister of several different congregations. For two years (1973–75), the American Board of Missions to Jews invited him to be the pastor of a church in Toronto, Canada. For the last ten years of his life he was minister of churches in Cincinnati, Ohio, USA. During this period he also wrote prolifically (being fluent in ten languages), and worked on a part-time basis for the 'Jews for Jesus' organization. He made such an impression that the chapel in the organization's headquarters in New York is dedicated to his memory. He was a disciplined scholar, preacher and worker. His legacies are the lives he touched, his books, a series of shorter writings and the organization called Messianic Literature Outreach, which he founded in 1979.

Rachmiel Frydland died from aggressive liver cancer in January 1985. One of the most widely read Christian periodicals in the USA published an obituary. It said:

Rachmiel and his wife Estelle with their four children

> Rachmiel Frydland, 65, survivor of the Nazi holocaust, Talmudic scholar, Jewish Christian movement in Israel, instructor in Judaica with Jews for Jesus; January 12, in Cincinnati.

This amazing life is almost dismissed with such a brief statement. His life story stands as witness to the horror of the Holocaust, and to the fact that it really happened. He was a witness to this history; but he was also a witness who could say with the apostle Paul, 'For I know that the sufferings of this present time are not worthy to be compared with the glory which shall be revealed in us (Romans 8:18).' His life preaching the gospel bears testimony to the fact that, however overwhelming the evil of mankind may seem, God has sent a Saviour to bring hope and assurance that this life and its suffering are not the end.

More Information on Rachmiel Frydland

His main writings are:

1. *A Hebrew Christian Looks at Israel.* Newark, New Jersey, USA. 1966.

2. *When Being Jewish was a Crime.* Thos. Nelson Inc. 1978, reprinted by Messianic Publishing Co. 1998 (ISBN 0–917842–01–4).

3. *What the Rabbis Knew about the Messiah.* Columbus, Ohio, USA. Messianic Publishing Co., 1991.

His numerous shorter writings are distributed in many languages by Messianic Literature Outreach, P.O. Box 37062, Cincinnati, Ohio 45222, USA.

My thanks are expressed to Marcy Kotting of Messianic Literature Outreach. She was extremely helpful in tracking down information and photographs about Rachmiel Frydland.

I would like to put on record that Rachmiel Frydland's daughter, Judith, was very cooperative and supplied several useful images of her father.

Cyril J. Barton: Bomber pilot

As Friday, 31 March 1944 dawned, sixty-one-year-old miner George Heads set off with a friend to join the early shift at Ryhope Colliery, near Sunderland, in the north-east of England. He was not to know that he had only a very short time left to live. Disaster was imminent.

To understand this, the clock must be wound back to 10.12 p.m. (22.12) on the previous evening, when Halifax bomber serial number LK797 had been given the green light to take off from RAF Burn, near Selby in Yorkshire, the home base of 578 Squadron. This marked the start of a long flight deep into Nazi Germany.

The Halifax pictured here is the type of heavy bomber flown by Cyril Barton on the Nuremberg Raid

Flying Officer Cyril Barton and his crew of six had already been through this routine half a dozen times before in the Halifax Mark III, which the crew had nicknamed 'Excalibur' after King Arthur's magic sword. The 'art' on the nose of their Halifax featured the sword striking through clouds into a burning Nazi swastika. For the aircraft's captain, Cyril Barton, this would be his nineteenth sortie over Germany, several of them to Berlin and back.

That night they were due to attack Nuremberg with a load of incendiary bombs. The crew would have known that the bombing mission on which they were embarking was a very hazardous one, since the German enemy was by now extremely efficient in

*The wreckage of the crashed aircraft
in the yard of Ryehope Colliery*

shooting bombers out of the sky. The weather conditions on that particular night made the raid even more dangerous than usual, as the vapour trails made by nearly 800 bombers could easily be seen by night fighters and anti-aircraft gunners.

Every man who flew in an RAF bomber, which obviously included Barton's crew, was highly trained and had volunteered for this role. However, none of the crews scheduled to go on the Nuremberg Raid could possibly have known that there had been serious disagreement among their senior officers. Much of the information available to the most senior commanders of Bomber Command indicated that it should be aborted, but the most senior officer of all, Air Chief Marshal Sir Arthur Harris, had overruled the objections. The decision was made: the Nuremberg Raid would take place.

From the point of view of RAF Bomber Command pilots, two principles were hammered home: the first was that they were to press on to the target if at all possible; the second that they must bring the precious bomber back, however adverse the circumstances.

Cyril Barton and his crew were about seventy miles (112 km) short of their target when they were hit by cannon fire from a Junkers 88 night fighter. The Halifax sustained serious damage, especially when a Messerschmitt 210 joined the fight against them. The tail guns and the mid-upper guns were put out of action, leaving the Halifax without any defences. One engine had failed, and two fuel tanks were punctured, fortunately without resulting in a fire. In addition, the internal communication system within the bomber was cut.

In the confusion of the battle, the navigator, wireless operator and bomb aimer all wrongly thought that instructions had been given to bail out. They consequently took to their parachutes, and all three were destined to spend the remainder of the war in German prison camps.

Barton was now in serious trouble. Nobody would have blamed him if he had dropped his bombs anywhere, perhaps in open fields, and tried to return home. Instead he made the decision to continue the mission, even though he risked having the silhouette of the plane illuminated by fires in the target area. If that happened he knew the night fighters would attack.

Without either a navigator or a bomb aimer, he reached his target and released the bombs himself. This in itself was an astonishing achievement. After finishing that part of the mission virtually unaided, he faced about four and a half hours of flying into head winds to return to England. Only three of the four engines were functioning and he had lost an estimated 400 gallons (1818 litres) of fuel. He had no navigator to guide him home and no wireless operator, even if the radio had been working. So Barton did all the navigating himself, possibly supplementing his pilot's maps with glimpses of the North Star, when it was visible.

While over the North Sea, the three remaining crew members threw out all movable equipment. The lighter the aircraft, the less fuel it would use. Eventually, in what had been an epic flight accomplished with only minimal guidance, they crossed the coast about ninety miles north of their home base. Barton could have had little or no idea where he was, but the Halifax in fact crossed into England at Ryhope, a small mining village about three miles south of the centre of Sunderland.

The fuel supply now failed completely. Barton ordered the remaining crew to take up crash positions near the wing spar of the Halifax. Directly in his path were four rows of miners' cottages. Fighting to maintain some control, he lifted the nose of the bomber to clear the cottages, hopefully to save lives. By taking that brave action he lost control of the aircraft, which by now was doing little more than gliding into disaster. 'Excalibur' crashed into the yard of Ryhope Colliery. All three crew members who were in crash positions survived the ordeal. However, on the ground flying debris from the doomed aircraft killed winding engineer George Heads who had been walking to work. Inside the crumpled cockpit lay the only member of the crew to die that night—twenty-two-year-old Cyril Barton.

The verdict of subsequent historians on this bombing mission was that it was the most disastrous of the Second World War. Ninety-five bombers failed to return and more men died in that one raid than Fighter Command lost in the whole of the Battle of Britain. John Terraine called this operation the 'black night' of the RAF in World War II. The Nuremberg Raid was not just a setback. It was a defeat.

The Victoria Cross, awarded posthumously to Cyril Barton, is Britain's highest award for bravery

In June 1944 it was announced that Cyril Barton had been awarded the Victoria Cross, the highest award for conspicuous bravery in the British armed services. The citation ended with these words:

> In gallantly completing his last mission in the face of almost impossible odds, this officer displayed unsurpassed courage and devotion to duty.

He was the only pilot of a Halifax to be awarded the VC—in his case not only for gallantry in the face of the enemy, but for acts of extreme bravery. But, as his mother remarked, 'It will not bring him back.'

Childhood and Family Life

Cyril Barton was born in 1921, which means that at the outbreak of the Second World War, in 1939, he was eighteen years old. His father was an electrical engineer who worked long hours, and his mother was fully occupied in the upbringing of five other children. Ken and Roy were born in the 1920s and Cynthia, Joyce and Pamela were all born in the 1930s. Together they were a happy, united family. But for them, as for many families, the inter-war years, a period of economic depression on both sides of the Atlantic, were financially difficult.

For instance, Cyril would have liked to play the piano, but there was no money for lessons or space in the house for an instrument even if they could have afforded one. The best he could do to indulge his musical interests was to teach himself to play the mouth organ and an old piano accordion. His holidays were usually spent with his grandparents in Dawlish, Devon. For ordinary working people in those days there was no question of flying away to the sun!

An old blurred image of the 'Barton Petrol Bowser' provides an example of the ways in which youngsters made their own entertainment during the inter-war years. The boys had seen a real petrol tanker on the main road, so, with an old oil drum, a soapbox and four pram wheels obtained from a local scrap dump, they created their own copy with the word 'SHELL' daubed on it.

Cyril (right) with his brothers Ken and Roy

Mrs Barton often related a story concerning an occasion when her husband plucked a chicken. Cyril, who was only five years old at the time, pushed the feathers into the sleeves of his pullover and jumped off the coal-shed roof in an attempt to fly.

Cyril left Beverley Boys' School, New Malden, Surrey, in 1935, aged fourteen, and secured a job as an apprentice design draughtsmen with Parnall (Aircraft) Ltd. at Kingston upon Thames. He was fortunate to be able to attend Kingston Technical College on day release in order to study for a National Certificate in Aeronautical Engineering.

Many teenage boys are fascinated by aircraft, and Cyril was no exception. One of his sisters recalls him taking her to an air display which featured a biplane and a wing walker to add to the excitement. He made no secret of his ambition to learn to fly. This was long before the threat posed by Hitler became clear.

Two images of Cyril as a teenager have survived. One shows him holding his first model aircraft made of balsa wood and tissue paper. Another photograph was taken in the Suffolk countryside when he was seventeen. He was visiting friends and relatives who lived in the area.

Cyril Barton was a clever and talented young man. If he had been given greater opportunities in his early life and had been able to go to university, who knows what he might have become? But he seems to have been happy with his life as it was, never complained and was proud of his family.

A model plane built and proudly displayed by Cyril when in his teens

In many ways the eldest son of a family like the Bartons would play an important role in the lives of his younger brothers and sisters. A lot of responsibility fell on him, with his father out at work all day, working long hours for modest pay, and his mother busy with household chores, making sure that the whole family was fed and well cared for.

Fifty years after he lost his life, Cyril's three sisters recorded their memories of him when he was young. The sisters all agreed that he was happy, bubbly, humorous—and constantly whistling. 'He was always doing things to amuse others.' When he was at home the house was 'full of fun and laughter. Cyril was lively, boisterous and a terrible tease. We all adored him.'

Cynthia remarks that though Cyril and Ken were such good friends they had totally different personalities. Cyril was 'the noisy extrovert, whereas Ken was shy and quiet'. When Cynthia was young, she desperately wanted a bicycle, so Cyril and Ken found an old frame on a rubbish dump. They cleaned it up and painted it blue, with the logo of 'Minnie Mouse' on the frame and handlebars. That was copied from the first of many Disney films that the brothers had taken her to see. Cyril might well have wanted to

occupy himself in his own way, and could have seen a younger sister as a nuisance. Instead, he spent hours teaching her to ride the bicycle.

Joyce too remembers Cyril as always having time for his young sisters. For instance, he taught her simple handicrafts and gave her basic lessons in how to sketch. 'He taught me to read,' she recalls, 'and bought me a book entitled *The Adventures of a Ten Shilling Note—* my first little book.'

Pamela picks out his serious side and speaks of his strong Christian faith. Keen to encourage his little sisters, he bought Bibles for Cynthia and Joyce on their eighth birthdays. But Pam received hers for her seventh birthday, because

This photograph of Cyril was taken in the Suffolk countryside while he was visiting relatives in 1938

he knew that he was about to go on operations over enemy territory and that he might not still be alive by her eighth birthday, as indeed proved to be the case. That Bible, given to her on 17 August 1943, remained Pam's most precious possession for the rest of her life.

The Air Force

Cyril Barton enlisted in the Royal Air Force Volunteer Reserve (RAFVR) in April 1941. His father, who had known the worst of trench warfare during the First World War, was understandably not very enthusiastic about his son's decision, but eventually he supported Cyril's wish. Soon after joining up, Cyril Barton sailed for North America, where he was recruited into the Arnold

Flying Training Scheme, named after the far-sighted US General 'Hap' Arnold. Only the very best men fulfilled the demands of this course. Many failed, or were 'washed out', as the men put it. Barton graduated as a Sergeant Pilot on 10 November 1942. A great deal of his initial training was carried out on an American Stearman biplane. In his words, it was a 'joy to fly'. His advanced training was completed at Napier Field, Alabama, on another American aircraft—the AT-6 Texan low wing monoplane, known in the RAF as the Harvard. He proved to be an exceptionally gifted pilot on all the aircraft he flew.

10 November 1942. Cyril graduates as a Sergeant Pilot in the USA

He was to retain happy memories of his time in the south of the US in general, and Alabama in particular. Indeed, American hospitality made a lasting impression on all the Barton family. During his training, Cyril became ill with bronchitis and spent some weeks in hospital. An American family took him under their wing and kept the family at home informed of his progress. The relationship between the two families continued long after the war was over.

By early 1943 Barton was back in Britain ready to complete his training and choose his crew. This was done at RAF Kinloss, in Scotland. His crew consisted of Len Lambert (navigator), Jack Kay (wireless operator), Freddie Brice (rear gunner), Wally Crate (bomb aimer), Harry Wood (mid-

Cyril chose these men as his crew

upper gunner) and Maurice Trousdale (flight engineer). All of these men were totally united in loyalty to their captain. Navigator Len Lambert wrote some memories of their time at Burn:

> We got very close together. Cyril Barton and I and the rest of the crew too. We went to the local Methodist Church and we were befriended by the Websters who had a farm near the airfield. They used to invite us over for supper on a Sunday after church and it was they who christened us 'Barton's Barmy Bomber Boys'. Mrs Webster would make these big apple pies. She had the pastry cut out 'BBBB'. The Websters were always at the end of the runway to wave us off when we went away.

> Cy Barton was a very competent pilot. He was strict in his ideas about the way things ought to be done, but he had a nice, easy-going way of putting it over. For example, when we were using the intercom system in the aircraft, we always had to use the absolute minimum of words. It had to be 'pilot to navigator', or 'navigator to pilot', just what we had to say, no chatter or anything else. We had to concentrate on what we were doing. There was a lot of hard work required. Our lives depended on it.

It was no surprise to his crew that after twelve raids Cy Barton was commissioned as a Pilot Officer on 5 January 1944.

Almost all narratives of the life of Cyril Barton describe his rank as that of Pilot Officer. The inscription on his gravestone, however, correctly refers to him as a Flying Officer. This apparent discrepancy is explained by the fact that he was promoted to Flying Officer on 26 March 1944, just a few days before his final mission. On the night of the fateful raid he was in fact a Flying Officer, although it is uncertain whether the news of this promotion had reached either him or his Wing Commander.

Christian Faith

No accurate account of the life of Cyril Barton would be complete if it omitted any reference to his Christian faith. Rev. Frank Coulquhoun, who was curate of St John's Parish Church in New Malden, Surrey, from 1935 to 1939, knew Cyril very well in those years and observed how he was maturing as a Christian over that period. Coulquhoun maintained his links with Barton right up to the time when he had the sad duty of conducting Cyril's funeral service in his home church in New Malden, and then the interment at Kingston Cemetery.

Coulquhoun first met Cyril in 1935, when he was about to leave school. The minister soon saw that for this young lad Christianity was something that went much deeper than mere attendance at Bible classes and church services. His faith was not just a question of keeping the outward rituals of the church. It was a personal commitment to Christ. Nor was it a purely theoretical faith. Colquhoun says that he had tested that faith by experience.

Cyril had heard the Christian gospel clearly presented. He knew that to be a real Christian involved a personal faith in Christ as Saviour and Lord. God had done a work in his heart which had given him a new nature and transformed him into a totally dedicated Christian. As a result, he was well known among his friends as someone who was definitely a Christian.

Although Barton's life had been transformed as a result of his faith in Christ, he remained a person who disliked sanctimonious talk and hypocrisy. There was nothing self-righteous about him. In no way did he put himself on a pedestal or see himself as being better than other people because of his Christian faith. He was perfectly natural, full of humour and fun, keen on sport and mad about flying. But for all that, Christ came first.

While he was based at RAF Burn, he shared sleeping quarters with the two other officers on the crew, Jack Kay and Wally Crate. Both were brave, kind men but they did not share his personal faith. Barton wanted some private time to read his Bible and pray. The need for these quiet spiritual moments with two of his crewmates present genuinely stressed him. He had a greater fear of carrying out his spiritual devotions in front of others who did not share a similar faith than he had of fighting the enemy! Letters to a friend in Kingston preserved by Colquhoun give an insight into Cyril Barton's inner life. Describing one occasion, a section of the letter says:

> I have been in some tight corners over Germany (and I am not shooting

a line. I really have!), but my heart never dropped with such a bump as when the door opened. I never felt so lonely in my life. I was in a cold sweat. Wally made no comment, but tip-toed round the room until I had finished reading the Bible and praying.

Once his two crew members realized that these quiet times were precious to him, the radio was turned off and chatter stopped during those moments. Barton's life of faith was accepted and respected by these two men who knew him better than almost anyone else. Elsewhere in the letter Barton told his friend in Surrey, 'The Lord is very real to me.'

Before he was posted to RAF Burn, he knew that he would soon be going on his first mission over Nazi territory. So he gave his brother Ken a letter, dated 18 July 1943, to be handed to his mother in the event of his death. This is what he wrote:

BUCKINGHAM PALACE

The Queen and I offer you our heartfelt sympathy in your great sorrow.

We pray that your country's gratitude for a life so nobly given in its service may bring you some measure of consolation.

George R.I.

The standard letter from King George VI which all families dreaded to receive

Dear Mum

I hope you never receive this but I quite expect you will. I am expecting to do my first operational flight in a few days. I know what 'ops' over Germany mean and I have no illusions about it. By my own calculations the average life of a crew is twenty 'ops' and we have thirty to do in our first 'tour' ...

At this point he refers to the money he had been saving up, and reveals that he had intended to use it on a university course after the war. He states that in the event of his death, any money was to be used as seemed appropriate.

From: Air Chief Marshal Sir Arthur Harris, K.C.B., O.B.E., A.F.C.

           Air Officer Commanding-in-Chief, Bomber Command.

27th June 1944.

My dear W. Barton

    I write to inform you that His Majesty The King has been graciously pleased to confer upon your son the Victoria Cross.

    I ask you on behalf of Bomber Command, and for my own part especially, to accept our sympathy in your loss.

    I hope, however, that this loss will be to some extent mitigated by the manner of your son's passing and by his high award, so well deserved, so hardly won.

    Your boy set an example of high courage and, finally, of extreme devotion to duty towards his crew, which will go down to history in the annals of his Service and shine as an inspiration for all who come after him.

    I hope indeed that a rightful pride in his achievements and his conduct will be of some consolation to you and yours at this time.

yrs. very sincerely

Arthur T. Harris.

F.J. Barton Esq.,
171 Elm Road,
New Malden,
Surrey.

*This personal letter from 'Bomber' Harris informs the family
that Cyril has been awarded the Victoria Cross*

Then he carries on:

> I am quite prepared to die. Death holds no terrors for me. I know I shall survive the Judgement because I have trusted in Christ as my own Saviour. I've done nothing to merit glory, but because He died for me it's God's free gift … All I am anxious about is that you and the rest of the family also come to know Him. Ken, I know already does. I commend my Saviour to you.

> Love to Dad and All

> Your loving son
> Cyril

On his return from flying training in America, Barton had met Doreen, the love of his life, in January 1943. She was from Harrogate in Yorkshire, not very far from his base. Had Hitler's war not intervened, there is little doubt that they would have married. Doreen also received a letter, written at about the same time as the one addressed to his mother. Doreen, who evidently shared his faith in God, had given him a book called *Daily Light*, a collection of Bible verses for reading each day. One verse in particular seems to have meant a great deal to both of them. He tells his mother that the words encourage him and that they are true. The Bible text to which he refers is Romans 8:28, which reads: 'We know that all things work together for good to them that love God.' These words express the profound faith that motivated Cyril Barton's life and they are quoted on his gravestone.

Perhaps the words of his sister Joyce, in all their childish simplicity, put it best. The family had just received the news of his death and her mother was weeping. Trying to console her, Joyce said, 'Don't cry, Mummy; he has only gone to live with Jesus.'

Flying Officer C. J. Barton, VC, is buried in the cemetery at Kingston-upon-Thames, Surrey

Cyril Barton would have agreed with that.

More Information on Cyril Barton

Martin Middlebrook's book *The Nuremberg Raid* is a readable and well-researched account of the mission. It explains precisely why the German anti-aircraft defences were so effective at the time, and includes more detail on all aspects of the raid than it is possible to mention here.

My contacts with Cyril Barton's sisters Joyce and Cynthia have been a joy. They have provided information and images unavailable from any other source. Particularly interesting is a short booklet called *Cyril Joe Barton, VC*, by W. W. Lowther published in 1994 jointly by Wearside College and Sunderland Leisure, Libraries and Arts. ISBN 0–905108–25–6. The bibliographical references in the Wikipedia article on the Internet, though giving almost no new information, are relevant.

The reference to historian John Terraine is from page 557 of the Wordsworth edition of his book *The Right of the Line*. This is a superb account of the role of the RAF in the European War from 1939 to 1945.

Rev. Frank Coulquhoun, MA, wrote a booklet largely about Cyril Barton's spiritual interests, to which he gave the title *The Air Pilot's Decision*. A copy of this is in the archives of the RAF Museum, Hendon. This is also the location of the Victoria Cross which Barton's parents received in Buckingham Palace from King George VI. Mrs Barton carried the medal in her handbag for the rest of her life, but after her death it was transferred to Hendon and is on permanent exhibition there.

7

Horst Alexander:
Prisoner for a reason

I t was bitingly cold, damp and still. Horst Alexander threw himself desperately onto the ground. Pushing his face into the wet grass of a field, he covered his head with his arms in an attempt to shrink himself into as small a target as possible. The threat of death from jagged pieces of shrapnel tearing into him seemed unavoidable. Each successive salvo of British mortar shells came closer to his small company of German soldiers.

Suddenly the shelling stopped. There was a strong smell of cordite in the air. The silence was broken only by the cries and moans of wounded cattle in the field. Feeling stiff and cramped, he struggled to his feet. It was dark and very foggy. Through the early morning gloom, Horst and his comrades now observed soldiers coming towards them. They hoped that they were German paratroopers. However, their hopes were dashed. These men were British infantry and they were advancing quickly. Horst had no chance to reach for his weapon, which was still lying on the ground where he had thrown it when the shelling began. The British soldiers called out for them to surrender.

While the British troops rounded up their prisoners, one man, who was about 100 yards (91 metres) away from Horst, broke away and ran to avoid capture. Horst heard fire from sub-machine guns. The runaway was hit and seriously wounded. The next time anybody saw him he was being driven away for medical treatment.

And so Horst became a prisoner of war, at about 5.00 a.m. on 5 November 1944. Other German forces were speedily retreating eastwards. Horst had been part of a rearguard posted alongside a railway track which ran just outside the Dutch city of 's-Hertogenbosch. This city in the southern Netherlands is often referred to as Den Bosch. A famous Dutch artist called Hieronymus Bosch died there in 1516 and ever since his name has been associated with the place. Horst, however, would from now on remember it for another reason altogether.

The years before his capture

Horst was born in February 1927 in Barmen, now part of the German industrial centre of Wuppertal. His father was a policeman and a member of the Nazi party. Horst himself, though at school from 1934 to 1944, was a member of the Hitler Youth. In this organization he underwent indoctrination in National Socialist ideology. One day in 1941 Horst went to visit his father at the police station, where he observed a man wearing a large yellow star on his jacket. With some reluctance his father informed the curious fourteen-year-old that the man was a Jewish cobbler, and that Jews had to report regularly to the police station.

After his schooldays ended, early in 1944, he served in the Reichsarbeitsdienst (RAD), or Reich Labour Service. This was started in 1935 to give employment to young German boys and girls. At first they were used as menial labour, helping to build roads or drain ditches, or even working on farms. As the Second World War began to affect Germany itself, these otherwise unemployed young people, now saturated with Nazi ideals, found themselves receiving military training. By the time Horst joined the RAD, he was one of many who were used to clear away rubble after Allied bombing, mostly in the industrialized Ruhr area. After his compulsory service with the RAD ended in June 1944, he became a soldier. His military career was to last for only five short months.

Arrival in England

In March 1945 Horst and his fellow prisoners were shipped to England by the Ostend to Tilbury route. Horst stepped ashore in England on a pleasant spring morning, marred only by the distinctive wailing noise of the British air-raid sirens and the distant explosion as one of Hitler's revenge weapons, probably a V-2 rocket, struck London, no doubt killing yet more civilians.

The captured Germans were surprised to be interviewed by British soldiers who spoke German as fluently as they did themselves. These men were in fact German Jews who put the knowledge of their mother tongue to good use in the Allied cause.

After the surrender of Germany in May 1945, the Allies forced German prisoners to watch films of the concentration camps. Now they learned that Nazi ideology had led to brutal and loathsome results. Horst's ideals broke down. Being an intelligent man, he started searching the writings of earlier German thinkers. He studied the philosophers Kant and Schopenhauer in particular.

Many prisoners had expected their captors and guards to be cruel and vindictive. But the treatment meted out to Horst and his companions was humane, even kind, at a time when the British might well have desired revenge against German troops.

While a prisoner at Featherstone Park Camp, Haltwhistle, in the north-east of England, during the summer of 1946, Horst received a letter from his father in Germany. It contained grim news. He already knew that his older brother had been killed in action in April 1942. Now he was to learn that his mother, his sister and her little son, Axel, had been killed in April 1945 during bitter fighting as the Soviet army invaded Germany. The only members of his family who survived the Second World War were Horst and his father.

The Wirral Peninsula

On 11 December 1946 Horst was moved to a small camp holding about 120 prisoners in Nissen huts at Clatterbridge, near Bebington in the middle of the Wirral peninsula. This is near to Merseyside in the north-west of England. The Germans worked on local farms and did other general labouring work. For instance, they dismantled unused Nissen huts that had been erected on the estate of Lord Leverhulme at Thornton

German prisoners were housed in Nissen huts like these

Hough during the war years. The use of these men for such tasks was necessary because many British men were away serving in the army, mostly in Germany.

The prisoners were not thought of as a threat, so they were lightly guarded. They were given second-hand British army uniforms to wear. These uniforms were dyed deep brown, which was not like the standard issue khaki. Also, a blue or red-coloured patch was stitched onto the back of the jacket and onto one of the trouser legs. The local civilians knew perfectly well that the Germans living among them were prisoners of war. One Bebington resident consulted by the author still has clear memories of a column of these German prisoners, all in their distinctive garb, marching through the old village of lower Bebington.

There was a church building in Bebington which had the word 'BETHESDA' displayed prominently over the front entrance. Horst had noticed it several times. At Christmas time in 1946 an invitation was received at the camp. It said that anybody who wished to go to Bethesda Hall for a cup of coffee (rather than tea, which would

Bethesda Hall seen in 2015. German prisoners visited this church by invitation at Christmas 1946

have been more usual) should come at 5.00 p.m. on Friday, 27 December. Any prisoner interested in taking up the invitation had to give his name to the camp clerk. Eleven men, including Horst, did this.

On the Friday concerned, to Horst's amazement, no less than eighty prisoners turned up. Extra tables, benches and cups and saucers were quickly arranged to cope with the unexpected numbers. Coffee and cakes were served in what seemed like abundance, even though food rationing was still in force. The men sang German Christmas carols. The prisoners were surprised and puzzled to find that the couple who had issued the invitation, a Mr and Mrs Benigson, addressed them in fluent German.

Remembering that day, Horst wrote:

> We were a company of men who for years had to live behind barbed wire … suddenly we found ourselves sitting in English church rooms at tables laid for all of us, and being attended to by very kind civilians who just under two years before had been our opponents in a terrible war.

On the way back to the camp at Clatterbridge the men discussed this strange visit to a church. Some thought it was an attempt to exert religious influence on men who had lost their confidence in Nazi beliefs. They said that they would not go again, even though they had enjoyed the hospitality. Others, like Horst, wanted to know more about Bethesda. What did the name stand for? The building did not look like a typical English parish church. One of the prisoners who came from Hamburg claimed that the Benigsons spoke German with a Hamburg accent. How was this possible?

The Truth about the Benigsons

Gradually, as visits to the church became more frequent, a nucleus of the prisoners found out that Mr and Mrs Benigson were in fact as German as they were, and that on coming to Britain, they had changed their surname to one that sounded more like an English name. Whether this was done legally or they adopted an alias is uncertain. Horst never knew or chose to find out such details.

Horst's memories continue:

> Now a further fact shattered us severely. Mr Benigson is a Jew, an academically trained engineer who had owned an electrical appliance company in Hamburg. In 1938 he and his wife had been driven out of Germany because he was a Jew. A number of his relatives had been killed in German concentration camps. In 1946 members of his family could be found on lists of missing persons … I myself was an eyewitness of Mr Benigson embracing a German prisoner of war … here again I had a question: how could he act in that way? From where did he receive the strength to meet this man in that way? After all, the prisoners fought for a régime and a people that caused indescribable sorrow to the Jews.

Only weeks after that first visit in December 1946, Mr Benigson told Horst that before the First World War he had served in the German Army which was loyal to the Kaiser. One of his superiors was General Georg von Viebahn. This officer was known among the troops as a practising Christian and an occasional preacher. While listening to his preaching, Mr Benigson was led to personal faith in Jesus Christ as the Son of God. Horst speculated: could this explain his inward attitude towards the prisoners?

Horst asked if he could have a personal talk with Mr Benigson. He continues his account as follows:

> I noticed that all the people in this Bethesda community had a personal relationship with Jesus Christ and that they knew about the forgiveness of their sins. To me it was like a miracle that this had developed among these Christians. It attracted me. On the other hand, my own pride would not allow me to submit myself to ideas like forgiveness, grace or mercy. For some time I rejected the gospel as it is described in the Bible. Mr Benigson, however, talked to me in simplicity about the grace and mercy of Jesus Christ … then on 13 January 1947 in his small kitchen at 4 Bethany Crescent, Bebington, I was finally able to throw overboard all my pride and arrogance and to entrust myself to God, who had created heaven and earth, but also in his inexplicable love went to the cross in the person of Jesus Christ, where he displayed the

proof of his love, including love to me. Getting up from my knees, Mr and Mrs Benigson gave me a big hug … thanks to the grace of my Lord and Saviour I was allowed to call myself a child of God.

Ever since I consider this day as the day of my rebirth. A reborn Jew led me, a Gentile, to faith in the Lord Jesus. To me without doubt this was decreed by the Lord and all that is left to me is to praise his love and grace. In fact, from this moment on I knew why I had become a prisoner of war in England.

Other prisoners besides Horst wanted to continue the friendships begun on that Friday after Christmas in 1946. The Benigsons' small house in Bethany Crescent was often crowded with German prisoners who enjoyed the friendly atmosphere. Horst himself started to worship regularly at Bethesda, which was linked to a Christian group called the Open Brethren.

Horst used his free time well. He walked to Port Sunlight model housing estate, built by Lord Leverhulme for the workers in his Sunlight soap factory. The eminent manufacturer had also built the Lady Lever Art Gallery in memory of his wife. This is still full of important works of art.

This recent photograph of 4 Bethany Crescent, Bebington, shows the house in which Horst came to faith

One day Horst was exploring the art on display when he found himself in the same room as the aristocratic Lord Leverhulme. Two assistants seemed to be bowing a little. Horst felt out of place in his prisoner-of-war garb, so he too made a few bows, not knowing what else to do in the circumstances. As he left the

In his off-duty time, Horst often walked to the Lady Lever Art Gallery in Port Sunlight

Art Gallery he saw a green Rolls Royce. This was Lord Leverhulme's personal means of transport!

Five days before moving away from the Wirral, Horst had the opportunity to visit Liverpool's Philharmonic Hall to listen to a fine performance of Handel's *Messiah* conducted by Malcolm Sargent. It made such an impression on him that he kept the programme among his few souvenirs of England.

One of Horst's souvenirs from England was this programme about Handel's Messiah, 1947

Return to Germany

Horst Alexander was eligible for return to his own country from March 1948 onwards, but he voluntarily stayed in England until 9 June 1949, classified as an 'alien'. In August 1949 he started as a trainee in a German company dealing in and melting copper and copper ingots. In February 1990 he retired from the same company as an attorney.

His post-war life is that of an ordinary man with a successful career. He married Ruth in 1955 and they had two children, a boy called Jörg and a girl named Birgitt. Both the children married and had their own children, making Horst and Ruth happy grandparents.

After his personal conversion to faith in Jesus Christ, he committed himself, not only to his work, but also to serving God in any way open to him. In his local church he served as an elder and was treasurer for over thirty years. He led prayer and worship services all his life. One of his priorities was the distribution of bilingual Bibles among Jews in Germany. As he grew older, he continued to be responsible for Christian meetings among retired people.

Family holidays frequently included visits to
Clatterbridge and Bebington so that he could
renew fellowship with the people at Bethesda
who had been so influential in his early
Christian life. As the years went by, many of
them died, but their work had been done well.
Horst Alexander, is a man with a Nazi past
whose life was changed for ever by meeting a
Jewish Christian who was faithful to the Word
of God.

Horst and his wife Ruth visit a Bebington family in 1966. Their children Birgitt and Jörg are shown in this photograph.

More information on Horst Alexander

All the information in this account ultimately derives from Horst Alexander
himself. There is a brief account of his experience in a book called *The
Germans We Trusted* by Pamela Howe Taylor, published by Lutterworth
Press in 2003. ISBN 0–7188–3034–2

I also relied on a series of letters and emails from Horst which were
received between 2001 and 2004 in answer to questions put to him in
an attempt to amplify the basic story. Permission to use the information
obtained in this way was granted.

The *Bethesda Bulletin* issued between August and November 2000, edited
by Barbara Coffey (who, as a very little girl, lived next door to Mr Benigson)
is a useful source containing the record of Horst's spiritual experience
described in his own words.

Adrian Brink of Lutterworth Press supplied two images of Horst. One
shows him in the garden of a Mr Dumbell while still a prisoner of war.
The other depicts him with his family visiting Rosa and Bill McMillan at
Bebington in 1966. Unfortunately both pictures are of very poor quality.
Civilian cameras in post-war Britain were often box cameras which gave
poor results.

Marvin Michael: Wartime test pilot

By the age of thirty-nine Marvin Michael had first-hand experience of the huge risks involved in being a senior experimental test pilot. He had flown the main types of bomber used by the Americans in the Second World War, subjecting new aircraft to the rigorous testing which they required. In such a hazardous occupation there had inevitably been accidents and other serious incidents. He had survived them all. He had the satisfaction of knowing that by the time combat crews flew these aircraft in bombing raids over Germany and Japan, they were free from technical faults.

In addition, all his boyhood ambitions had come true. He owned his own aeroplane. He was well paid. His wife and children were healthy and gifted. People would often say to him, 'You must be a really happy man.' But he wasn't. Nor did he know why. He was restless and discontented. Sometimes he would ask himself, 'Is this all there is to life?' He was about to find the answer to his own question.

A Minister's Son

Rev. Howard Michael and his wife Elsie had three sons. Marvin, born in 1912, was the eldest and there were two younger brothers, Vernon and Herbert. It was a happy, well-integrated family, though they moved home several times in Marvin's early years as his father was called to work in churches in different parts of the US.

While the family was living in Garden City, Kansas, Marvin became obsessed by aviation and flying. In 1926, as a schoolboy of fourteen, he learned to drive a car. (In those days no licence was required). He left high school in 1929 and by 1932 he was a student at the University of Michigan studying aircraft design, though his ambition from the age of ten was to be a pilot.

In the summer of 1934 he made his first solo flight after only thirty-five minutes' tuition. Usually pilots require about twelve hours of teaching before they go solo, but Marvin had already flown a large number of hours in gliders. It was his considerable experience in flying sailplanes which enabled him to make the transition to powered flight so easily.

Marvin poses by his first aircraft, a Waco 9, in 1934

A Professional Pilot

In 1937 the University of Michigan sent Marvin an unexpected telegram. It said that he had been awarded a scholarship to study for a higher degree in the academic year 1937–38. At the end of these studies he would be qualified in both aerodynamics and aircraft engineering.

The next year, 1939, was a significant one in Marvin's life. He had met Laura Moser, a pretty English Literature teacher from Pennsylvania, some time earlier. She came from a Lutheran background but, for her as for Marvin, at this period of her life attending church was no more than a religious activity. On their second date, Marvin wanted to show off his piloting skills. They went flying in a light aircraft. Later he admitted that if she had been unenthusiastic about the flight, he would probably have lost interest in her! However, love blossomed, and they were married in April 1939. They were to have four children, Carol, Gwen, Mike and Larry. Their happy marriage lasted for sixty-four years.

The Impact of World War II

At the outbreak of the Second World War the United States was politically divided in its attitude to the war in Europe. At first many ordinary Americans were strongly of the opinion that the country should remain neutral, although most modern scholars think that President Franklin D. Roosevelt was secretly opposed to this position. All his political instincts were against the totalitarianism of the Nazis in Europe and also that of the rulers of Japan. By the summer of 1940, however, American attitudes had changed. An official book called *An Outline of American History* issued by the US Information Service contains this sentence: 'Very few US citizens were any longer neutral in thought.' Almost all Americans despised Hitler's attacks on smaller countries. They admired the British for the brave resistance they showed at the time of the Battle of Britain and for the fact that during most of 1940–41 Britain was the only country still actively fighting the Nazis.

The Second World War in Europe brought about major changes in the US aircraft industry. No longer would their priority be the development of civil aircraft. The US government led by President Roosevelt entered into massive contracts for the production and testing of all types of military aircraft.

A Change of Direction

In 1940 Marvin received a letter which was to change the direction of his life. It was from the Boeing Aircraft Company and arrived out of the blue. Signed by one of Marvin's boyhood heroes, an American test pilot called Eddie Allen, it read:

> We are expanding our flight department and have an opening for a combination aerodynamicist and flight test engineer. We can offer 250 dollars a month.
>
> Signed:
> Edmund T. Allen
> Chief of Flight and Aerodynamics

Marvin was ecstatic. All his previous experience in other aircraft companies seemed to have been in preparation for this moment.

The Boeing Company was based at Seattle in the state of Washington, in the far north-west of the United States. Within four weeks of receiving Eddie Allen's letter Laura and Marvin had moved there. Boeing had recently been awarded the first of many contracts for the mass production of a bomber called the B-17 Flying Fortress. At this

This aircraft, the Flying Fortress, was a type extensively tested by Marvin

point the US was still at peace. The Japanese attack on Pearl Harbor was still in the unknown future. Nevertheless, Marvin was soon involved in the high-altitude tests of this bomber, which was to play an important role in the war against Germany, and within a couple of years would be a common sight in the skies all over England, particularly East Anglia.

By the end of 1941 Britain was no longer on its own. With both the USSR and the United States being drawn into the conflict, it was now a war between the Allies on the one hand and Germany and Japan on the other. It was no longer a European war; it was a World War.

By 1942 one fifth of Seattle's population was working for Boeing. The factory operated three shifts, working round the clock, to manufacture B-17 Flying Fortresses and produced no less than a dozen aircraft every single day. The flight-test department was working flat out for seventy hours a week. High-altitude testing involved flying at nearly 40,000 feet and was not pleasurable; it was sheer hard work. Moreover, it was also always potentially dangerous.

Eddie Allen

At that time most American test pilots, including Marvin, looked on Eddie Allen as a role model. Though now largely forgotten, he had a string of major flying achievements to his credit. *Time* magazine published an article about him, in which he was described as 'the greatest test pilot aviation has ever had'. At the time it was probably true.

Test pilot Eddie Allen at the controls of a Flying Fortress

On 18 February 1943 Eddie, now aged forty-seven and at the peak of his skills, took the B-29 Superfortress on a test flight (this was the plane that was destined to drop the atomic bombs on Japan). Fires broke out in the engines and Eddie and the ten men with him died in the subsequent crash. There is a plaque in downtown Seattle which records the names of men who gave their lives in the Second World War. It includes these eleven men. The loss of test pilots and crews was just as much a wartime sacrifice as the death of others on active service in distant battle zones.

The Superfortress is the type of aircraft in which Eddie Allen lost his life. Later, Superfortresses dropped the atomic bombs on Japan in 1945.

Marvin was devastated. The man he had idolized for so long was dead. Laura reminded Marvin of the time they had a meal with Eddie and his wife Florence. The Allens spoke mostly about the dream house which they were building and furnishing for their retirement years. It was at

Encinitas, north of San Diego, California. Marvin and Laura had even been invited to see this extraordinary house by Eddie Allen's caretaker/botanist, Mr Rohn. Marvin recorded what Mr Rohn told them:

> For a good many years now, Eddie has been bringing back unique art treasures from all over the world for his retirement home. Mr Rohn also showed us every room, explaining the Gothic windows, beautiful furniture, and the sunken Roman living room. We admired the huge fireplace, the many original paintings from Italy, India and other places. We climbed the steep winding staircase, stopping to look at all the framed art along the way. Even the banister, made of intricately carved wood and wrought iron, was a work of art. At the top a door opened to a solarium filled with blooming roses, geraniums and begonias. We sat on the rattan furniture enjoying the view. From the top of the cliff one hundred feet above the ocean, we had a 180 degree view of pounding surf, rock strewn beach and passing ships on the horizon.

Marvin then added an interesting comment, which reveals his state of mind at the time: 'There in the sunshine, I was taken with this definition of success. I too wanted an opulent home with expensive art work. I wanted to be a millionaire and fly my own airplane everywhere. Laura and I went home full of such dreams about our future.'

A Narrow Escape

The Flying Fortress bombers needed to be flown to England so that they could be used in raids on Nazi Germany. To achieve this, extra fuel tanks were installed instead of bombs. On 13 March 1943 Marvin and his crew carried out a test on these tanks in which he made the B-17 dive until it reached a speed of 300 mph. This led to half the tail surface breaking off. The plane subsequently went out of control and could not be landed. Marvin and his crew only survived by bailing out. He had further life-threatening experiences testing the B-29 Superfortress, the plane which had already claimed the lives of Eddie Allen and his crew.

By 1951 the Second World War was over, but as the Cold War became more dangerous to world peace, Marvin was still testing bombers, in

Marvin at the controls of a Superfortress

particular the six-engine jet aircraft called the Stratojet. In the event of a nuclear war, these planes were designed to carry atomic bombs as far as the USSR should this become necessary. Marvin also did pioneering work in air-to-air refuelling, using a rigid boom to transfer fuel from a tanker plane to the receiving aircraft.

Is this all there is?

Friends and colleagues saw Marvin Michael as a gifted pilot and engineer. Not only that, but he was a churchgoer who sent his four children to Sunday school. In his own words:

> I didn't drink, smoke, swear or tell dirty stories … [but] … when I occasionally tried to read the Bible, it was hard to understand. My perfunctory prayers changed nothing. I knew something was wrong, but my struggles to find the cause were fruitless … I felt utterly frustrated. I was frequently worried and bitter over trivial things. Night after night sleep eluded me.

The doctor gave him sleeping pills, but Marvin remained weary. Then he started to have trouble staying awake at work, especially in the middle of the afternoon. So he went back to the doctor, who then prescribed Dexedrine to keep him awake and alert. Laura, however, questioned the wisdom of trying to solve whatever was wrong by taking tablets.

At this time some close friends invited Marvin and Laura to The Firs, a Christian conference centre about ninety miles north of Seattle. People from all over the north-west of the United States gathered there for weekend and week-long conferences. The aim was to hear the best Bible teachers available and discuss what was taught. Marvin wrote, '… what I heard started to bother me. Other people seemed happy. I sensed their joy and their commitment to God, and it made me feel uncomfortable. My uneasy feeling came with the realization that … I had just been *playing* church.'

One conference he attended was especially unsettling: 'I woke up at about four o'clock one morning and couldn't get back to sleep.' He went walking on his own among the fir trees. The words of Christ went through his mind: 'Come unto me, all ye that labour and are heavy laden, and I will give you rest.' Marvin reflected that he was carrying a heavy load, but was not experiencing the rest about which Christ spoke. Later, he wrote:

> Suddenly it came to me. If God exists—then my relationship to him is THE MOST IMPORTANT THING IN THE WORLD … Finally I said, 'Lord, you take my life and run it … I've been trying to run my life in my own strength.' At that very instant I felt as if a ton of lead was lifted abruptly from my shoulders. Tears of joy trickled down my face. My commitment to total obedience to God and his Word, the Bible, became the turning point of my life. This all sounds rather self-righteous, as though I'd arrived. Far from it! As a writer put it, 'Christians are not perfect—they're just forgiven.'

Continuing the theme Marvin added:

> What happened in that moment under the fir trees? I realized that when one ignores God's laws, the penalty is eternal separation from God. But in recognizing my transgressions, asking divine help … I was assured of God's forgiveness. God is sovereign and I don't understand why he planned the world as he did, but I don't have to understand. Gradually I came to realize that God loved me so much that he sent his Son, Jesus, to earth so that at the proper time in history he might die on a cross. His death paid the penalty for my transgressions so I can spend eternity in heaven with God. My sins were thereby pardoned. Earlier in my life, as a churchgoer I thought I had accepted God's forgiveness, and wondered why I had no real peace. But on that weekend at The Firs I realized what acceptance really meant. My regular church attendance was just religious activity …
>
> Under the fir trees that morning I totally surrendered to God's rule in my life. I hadn't understood what it meant to put my full trust in God … For

nearly thirty years I'd believed intellectually that Christ died for my sins, but I wasn't willing to trust him to direct my steps day by day. I had to make a total commitment; it was all or nothing. Now that I understood how vital it was, I could take that step.

In the following weeks I noticed a tremendous difference in myself, and I feel the change was obvious to others as well … the daily battle did not evaporate … I would stumble, but God's forgiveness was always there. From that moment on, however, I no longer needed sleeping or wake-up pills.

Involvement with MAF

Spiritual experiences such as the one that transformed Marvin Michael's life always have consequences. Back at work, a Boeing engineer named Ted Ayre asked Marvin if he had ever heard about Mission Aviation Fellowship (MAF). This brief conversation was to be the start of Marvin's long association with MAF. It also led to contact with Nate Saint.

Nate Saint (left) with his friend Marvin

Nate was a pioneering MAF pilot, working mostly in the Ecuadorian jungle. In November 1952 Nate, his wife Marj and their three children came to stay at the Michaels' home in Seattle. Nate was totally dedicated to using small single-engine aircraft to provide air transport for missionaries.

The first day of the visit, Marvin darkened one of the four small bedrooms so that Nate could show his home-made film called *Conquering Jungle Barriers*. This film opened Marvin's eyes to the scope of the work in Ecuador. The narration was spoken by Nate, who provided a clear insight into the value of aircraft to missionaries in isolated places. Since it was Nate's first visit to Seattle, Marvin had contacted the ministers of all the local churches with the aim of introducing Nate and his work. At all the churches, the film was shown. The aim was to make MAF better known and perhaps raise support.

At the end of the month, as the visit was drawing to a close, Nate asked Marvin to spend Christmas and New Year at MAF's base in Los Angeles. The Boeing factory was shut down over this period and Nate needed help with all sorts of administrative tasks. Laura, Marvin and the children drove to Los Angeles in order to help him.

One day Nate said to Marvin, 'I've got a brain storm that you can help me with. When missionaries are hacking their way through the jungle they sometimes get sick or run out of food. If I could let out a bucket on a long cord and trail it behind the plane, I could fly circles round the people on the ground, and by slowly decreasing altitude, maybe I could lower some medicine or food to the ground. As far as I know, this has never been tried. Let's go see if we can make it work.'

Nate and Marvin went to a discount shop and bought 1,500 feet of nylon cord and a canvas bucket, which they filled with oranges. Nate flew the single-engine plane in circles around Marvin, who remained on the ground. The bucket came lower and lower until Marvin caught it and removed the oranges. When Nate landed Marvin yelled, 'You did it, Nate. You did it.' As they were discussing this with their wives that evening, Marvin told Nate, 'I'm thrilled to have helped make it work.' Nate's invention had been in his mind for some time. With help, he tested it more until he was finally satisfied with the result.

On at least one occasion in Ecuador, a life was saved using this bucket-drop method. After the initial experiments Nate had refined the technique by installing a field telephone in the bucket. Missionary Frank Whiting, his wife and two

Nate Saint stands by the light plane he used to test his bucket-drop system

children had been on a three-day walk from their mission station in order to buy supplies and receive routine medical care. As they were on their way home, Nate made a point of flying over them in his MAF plane to make sure that they were safe. He saw that Frank's son David was lying on the ground. When Nate lowered the bucket with the telephone, Frank reported, 'David was bitten by a coral snake,' and asked, 'Can you bring us antivenin, please?' There was no time to lose. Coral-snake venom could be fatal in a short time. Nate's prompt action meant that within about forty-five minutes the youngster had the medicine which saved his life.

In 1955 Nate and four friends developed a plan to share the Christian message with the Huaorani people (also known as Aucas) who lived in a remote area of the Ecuador jungle and were known for their extreme violence. In order to establish a rapport with them, the bucket-drop system was used to deliver gifts as tokens of friendship showing the goodwill of the five men. Eventually, Nate landed his light plane on the beach of the Curaray River. After a brief meeting with some of the Huaoranis, he took one, nicknamed 'George', on a flight over his own village.

Sadly, on 8 January 1956 Nate and his four friends were all killed by Huaorani spears and the plane was vandalized. To this day the motives of the Huaoranis for this action are not clearly known because at first they had appeared to be friendly. The news media, including some of the Christian press, were very critical of the victims for risking their lives. Marvin's view was different: 'This was no tragedy. It was a glorious triumph in God's plan. Because of the example of five dedicated missionaries, who were willing to lay down their lives to take the gospel to the Aucas, thousands of men and women committed their lives to full-time Christian service.'

In the years following the death of Nate Saint and his friends, Marvin took regular meetings to promote the work of MAF (US). Often Marvin showed Nate's film *Conquering Jungle Barriers*, which enhanced interest. He became an official representative for MAF. For at least thirty-six years this connection with MAF provided, in Marvin's own words, 'adventure, challenge, and great spiritual rewards'.

Although he was still employed by Boeing, the firm was generous in granting him leave to fly on various mercy missions. The Marine Medical Mission, for instance, provided doctors and dentists for the native people of British Columbia. Marvin would often fly specialists to places where the need was greatest.

Mercy Airlift

After over thirty years working for Boeing, Marvin retired in 1972, aged fifty-nine.

It had been a demanding and fulfilling working life. Marvin thought hard and long how his retirement years ought to be spent. His earlier contact with Nate Saint provided the background to his decision to make a transition into work with Christian organizations. As Marvin saw it, all human life has a purpose, and the Lord had a plan for his life. So from 1972 he would commit himself full-time to supporting Christian causes.

Soon after retirement, he heard about an organization called Mercy Airlift, based in southern California. It had only been founded round about the time that Marvin retired. Its aircraft flew food and other supplies to starving people in Third World countries. Marvin submitted an application to be involved in its work. Because of his commitment to MAF he only

Ethiopians try to push a cow into a plane belonging to Mercy Airlift

offered to substitute for pilots who were on vacation. To his surprise Dr Mervin Russell, the president of Mercy Airlift, telephoned him at home to explain the serious nature of the current famine in Ethiopia. Two years earlier, one tribe had numbered around 5,000; now they were reduced to 1,200. He pleaded with Marvin to drop his other commitments and go to Ethiopia to help save as many lives as possible.

Marvin packed hurriedly and asked Laura to join him later. In May 1975 he flew Mercy Airlift's old transport plane from its base in California to Greenland. From there he flew to Iceland and then on to London. The next leg took the old aircraft via Cairo to Ethiopia in East Africa.

Marvin is pictured third from the left with some of his helpers during his time in Ethiopia 1975–77

The sad spectacle of human beings reduced to skin and bone and dying of malnutrition appalled Marvin. Before long he was put in charge of the whole operation to save lives. He determined to do what he could. Soon the elderly Dakota aircraft was in the air carrying food to a refugee camp. Hearing of the refugees' plight, tribesmen from another area insisted on pushing a live cow into Marvin's aircraft, along with other supplies! This animal would help to provide food for a few of them.

Laura and Marvin operated out of the Ethiopian capital city, Addis Ababa, for about two years. One Sunday morning in March 1977, Marvin was attending a service at the International Church in Addis Ababa when somebody tapped him on the shoulder. The administrator for the Sudan Interior Mission begged him to leave the service. He explained that a radio message had been received from Gode, south-east of Addis. It was an urgent request pleading for the plane to be sent immediately. A rapid response could possibly save the lives of up to thirty people.

Somali bandits had started a vicious armed attack in an attempt to steal money which they believed to be in the hands of the missionaries. Dr Donald McClure, who, as Marvin's chief helper, had been important in guiding his priorities, had been shot dead. Marvin flew right into the danger area in order to rescue as many people as possible. The trustworthy old plane was soon packed full. Everyone on board was frightened. The aircraft was so overloaded that the final take-off from the danger zone was little more than a calculated risk. Marvin wrote afterwards, 'We had flown into Gode against impossible odds and by the grace of God, we made it. In Africa I learned about heartbreak and challenge.'

Marvin was now sixty-five, a fairly common retirement age, when he was forced to evacuate from Ethiopia. As the work of Mercy Airlift expanded, Laura and Marvin followed it with interest. It was time for them to wind down from the dangers which they had faced in the turbulence of Ethiopia. Marvin was often heartbroken about the repeated famines and tragedies in Africa and other parts of the world. In his Memoir, he makes this observation about his work with Christian relief organizations: 'My reward was a joyful feeling of fulfilment, far beyond the satisfaction that my work as a Boeing test pilot had brought me.'

Reflections in Old Age

In his senior years Marvin thought about the people whose influence had most deeply affected his life. For instance, Eddie Allen had taught him several valuable lessons. Some were positive; one negative.

When the University of Michigan Scholarship Committee offered Marvin free tuition in the 1937–38 academic year, he felt the need for advice. What should he study? Eddie Allen's name sprung to his mind. Even though he doubted whether such an important man would take the trouble to answer an enquiry from a student, Marvin wrote to him anyway. He received a three-page hand-written reply. The advice was to obtain a master's degree in aerodynamics. Later, it was Eddie Allen who offered him his job at Boeing. No wonder Marvin respected him.

However, it was Eddie Allen who persuaded him that he needed a luxurious house and money beyond his needs. As a result of the accident to the prototype Superfortress, Eddie never lived to occupy his own splendid retirement home. Marvin thought how sad it was that his hero Eddie had not followed the teaching given by Jesus in what is often called the 'Parable of the Rich Fool'. This parable carries a powerful message. Consider what it says:

The ground of a certain rich man produced a good crop. He thought to himself, 'What shall I do? I have no place to store my crops.'

Then he said, 'This is what I'll do. I will tear down my barns and build bigger ones, and there I will store all my grain and my goods. And I'll say to myself, "You have plenty of good things laid up for many years. Take life easy; eat, drink and be merry."'

But God said to him, 'You fool! This very night your life will be demanded from you. Then who will get what you have prepared for yourself?'

This is how it will be with anyone who stores up things for himself but is not rich towards God.

(Luke 12:16–21, NIV).

Marvin also thought of his friendship with Nate Saint. He wrote:

When my spiritual growth became my guiding influence, I was destined to meet someone who was indeed well-named—Nate Saint. It was obvious to me from the time we met that here was a man who had a close walk with the Lord. During the few years I was privileged to be his friend I gained a great deal, not only in finding ways to use my flying skills for the glory of the Lord, but in learning to seek God's guidance continually in every aspect of my life.

Pursuing the theme of recollection, he wrote:

Another person whose influence was profound was Dr Donald McClure. He had given me the most helpful advice while I was in Africa. In Ethiopia I can still see the seventy-year-old carrying 100 pound sacks of cement up the sloping floor of our Mercy Airlift Dakota. Gracious, loving, generous, hospitable Dr McClure had started working in Africa fifty years earlier. I admired this veteran missionary as much as any man I knew. He was a tremendous inspiration to all who knew him and did not deserve to be killed by the Somali rebels.

Just as Marvin's life had been influenced by important people he met, so he endeavoured to spend his life in useful, caring purposes by influencing others. If he was invited to speak about MAF or Mercy Airlift in his retirement years, he would use any opportunity. Any church or group who would listen was an avenue of service. Sometimes he was asked to give his testimony, describing lessons he had learned from his flying experiences. These occasions were taken very seriously.

Both Laura and Marvin were active members of the Presbyterian Church. Marvin, who had musical gifts, sang in the choir. Laura also led a group which studied the Bible. This was an international organization called Bible Study Fellowship.

Both of them took their faith in God seriously. They were people of prayer, particularly relating to those whose efforts were to better the lives of people in Third World countries. As long as age and health permitted, Marvin remained a very active Christian. At the end of his autobiography he remarks that everything he did had the aim of bringing glory to God. Laura predeceased him, and Marvin died in August 2010, aged ninety-eight.

Marvin celebrated his 80th birthday by taking the controls of this light aircraft. Laura stands beside him.

More information on Marvin Michael

Marvin's autobiography, *A Passion for Flying*, was published in 1999 by Ambassador-Emerald International (ISBN 1–883893–59–3).

His daughter Carol Ortiz has kindly supplied most of the photographs with the exception of those listed below.

The Boeing Company archives supplied the high-resolution image of

Marvin Michael in 1943, and the photograph of Eddie Allen at the controls of a Flying Fortress.

MAF (Canada) supplied the photograph of Nate Saint standing by an aircraft.

There is a considerable range of books about what was then called 'Operation Auca' and its consequences. One of the most popular is *Through Gates of Splendour* by Elisabeth Elliot. The original 1957 edition has been reprinted regularly. ISBN 0–8423–7152–4/978–0–8423–7152–0.

Readers who are curious about how Mercy Airlift developed will find details on: www.mercyairlift.org